HOW TO LIVE LIKE A MILLIONAIRE ON AN ORDINARY INCOME

by STEVEN WEST
in collaboration with
Donald Tyburn-Lombard

For information, address
Aabbott McDonnell-Winchester Publishers
376 Wyandanch Avenue
North Babylon, New York 11704
(516) 643-3500

ISBN: 0-89519-002-8

© 1977 Aabbott McDonnell-Winchester

To my father, who gave me the inclination
To the Wharton School, who gave me the motivation
To Max and Ron, who taught me retailing
and to Sherri who gave me the inspiration

Written by...Steven West
in collaboration with.............Donald Tyburn-Lombard

Graphics Author........................William Alan Discount

Photography by ....Jim Hanson
and Vincient Busby

Research Directors....................................Robert Orgel
....Sandy Brotman
....Beverly Blake

TABLE OF CONTENTS

CHAPTER THREE
TIIE VISIBLE SYMBOLS OF SUCCESS... 47

How to obtain a suite of offices without paying rent
How to furnish your new offices without any cost
How to set up a legal corporation for under $100.00
How to obtain a legal and accounting braintrust free
How to obtain a luxury car without paying for it
How to publicize your new business at no cost
How to advertise your new business at lowest cost
How to get a luxury home without down payment
How to live in luxurious apartments at half the rent
How to enjoy luxurious vacations free and profitably
How to get VIP treatment from airlines and restaurants
How to use your new position to gain political power
How to get an office building named after your company
How to use limousines and aircraft to impress clients

CHAPTER FOUR
THE ART OF EMPLOYING CREDIT....... 91

How to earn 17% interest with very little risk
Understanding how the millionaires use credit
The important concept of using other people's money
How to gain control of a publicly held corporation
A simpler legal way to sell your own stock to the public
A system that makes money for everyone involved.
A case history of the legal takeover of a corporation
The simplest way to start saving money every today
How to get a good credit rating for your company
How to make friends with 100 successful people
How to smooth the way for instant supplier credit
How to get free credit information from your bank
How to raise cash and get a great employee too
How to raise money and get excellent suppliers

INTRODUCTION

Let's get something straight, right at the beginning. This book is real, it's honest; everything in it is legal and legitimate.

The title of this book is real. It means exactly what it claims. This book can teach you HOW TO LIVE LIKE A MILLIONAIRE ON AN ORDINARY INCOME. It can show you how—step-by-step to reach a position in whatever business community you choose—which will permit you to enjoy all of the outward trappings of the life of a millionaire and still do it on an ordinary income.

If you want to go further and actually become a millionaire in fact, instead of just living like one that's entirely up to you. It can be done but you'll have to work harder and for a longer period of time.

I know you can do either because I have achieved both goals. I started out to live like a millionaire and succeeded. Then, after a while I decided to actually become a millionaire.

That's exactly what I am right now—a self-made millionaire. As the controlling stockholder of several multi-million dollar corporations, I am the head of a multi-national organization. Some of my corporations are engaged in manufacturing world famous products such as Montessori Toys and other educational items. Other corporations own and operate nationwide chains of retail stores, pet shops, snack bars and boutiques.

There was a time when I was right where you are now. The only difference is that I didn't have the book you are now holding. That gives you a big advantage.

That's one of the reasons why—after I made my millions—I decided to write this book. There's nothing wrong with offering other people a chance at success and happiness.

The other reason is to make money—naturally. Samuel Johnson once said that a man who wrote a book without the expectation of making money was a blockhead. I'm not. I expect to make a lot of money with this book because it's real. There's never been another one like it. There still isn't. I know because I searched everywhere for a book like this when I started out.

I had to do it the hard way.

How did I hit on the idea? Oddly enough the first major breakthrough came to me during a performance of Arthur Miller's play "Death Of A Salesman". There was one scene in that play that hit me like a sledgehammer.

I'm sure you must have seen the play. It was made into an excellent motion picture with Frederic March playing Willie Loman. It was shown on TV a number of times. Do you remember the scene when Willie Loman falls to his knees and cries out to the ghost of his rich, successful brother-in-law, "Tell me the secret, Ben! Tell me how you did it!"

The ghost starts to speak and—I don't know about anybody else—but I leaned forward in my seat because I wanted to hear that answer as much as Willie Loman did.

The ghost starts to speak and, I don't know about what he said. Neither could Willie. The ghost faded away, still speaking softly and Willie and I were left without that precious secret of success.

That's when it hit me. Every book I'd read had claimed that it would reveal the secret of how to succeed but—just like Ben's ghost—they seemed to be telling me, but just faded away in cliches and platitudes. Often I was left with nothing but the feeling that I had been taken in by a slick sales promotion.

Sitting there in that darkened theatre, I realized that I had been looking in the wrong places for the answers I needed. Willie Loman had the right idea. The only people who could give me the right answers were the people who had become rich through their own efforts. They had the secret. They had the blueprint.

People like John J. Rockefeller, Andrew Carnegie, Bernard Baruch, Andrew Mellon—all rich men right up to Aristotle Onassis. They would provide the right answers. I began to read about their lives. I scoured the libraries—the newspaper files—for stories, interviews, things they've said. I was looking for some common denominators—things that they all had in common. I knew it was there—somewhere.

It took time, sweat and a lot of patient digging but I finally found what I was looking for—and a whole lot more. You'll get the full story in the next chapter. The point is—once I found what I was looking for, I began to build my own blueprint for success.

Remember, I just wanted to live like a millionaire I didn't want to actually be one. I had no intention of breaking my back and actually make a million dollars.

Well, the blueprint worked. I began to live the kind of life that any millionaire would have been satisfied with. It was the kind of life I used to dream about. Now I had it and then—something odd happened to me. I began to think like a millionaire. The more I thought that way the more convinced I became that I wouldn't be really happy until I actually became a millionaire.

So I stopped just playing the role and started to work and I mean really work at turning an illusion into a reality. I went at it full time and never stopped.

Well—here I am—rich, successful, happier than I've ever been in my life, doing what I like to do best. I intend to go right on working, building new companies, making more money, because I enjoy making money. The money game is the greatest game I know.

So, it's up to you. I can promise you that you or any other man or woman who wants to live like a millionaire on an ordinary income can do it—just by following the directions in this book.

If you want to go further—if you are willing to really dig in, and work harder than you ever have in your life then you really can make that first million—and a lot more.

It's entirely up to you. Everything you need to know—the entire blueprint is in your hands. All you have to do is read it, digest it, understand it, and you're on your way.

Speaking of understanding, I'd like to say something about the way this book is written. My good friend and associate, Donald Tyburn-Lombard, and I have both tried to write this book as simply and directly as the directions on a can of Campbell's Tomato Soup.

I don't like books that try to impress me. Neither does he. We both wanted a book that would teach you how to succeed in the simplest possible manner.

Another thing about this book is this: it is not designed to be read straight through at a single sitting. You can, if you want to, but there's a lot of material to absorb. Believe me when I tell you that you'll be much better off if you read it slowly—one chapter at a time—with plenty of thinking time in between.

This is no ordinary book. It will change your life in many ways no matter what you do after you've read it through completely. I can assure you that the change will be for the better. You will view yourself and the world you live in much differently than you do now.

The first chapter of this book—which I recommend that you read now—will give you the general idea of what you will have to do to achieve your goal of living like a millionaire on an ordinary income.

It will explain the 'answers' I found when I searched through the files on the lives of the 'rich,' and it will also give you some idea of the sequence of events that must take place as you start towards your goal.

In later chapters you will be given specific step-by-step instructions on how to acquire the basic material that are necessary to your new role in life.

Be sure to have a pen or pencil handy as you read the first chapter. If there is anything that you do not understand then underline the sentences or place a bracket around the paragraph but mark it so that you can come back to it when you have finished reading the first chapter. If you have trouble understanding (even after re-reading) write to me (care of the publisher). I'll try to get back to you as quickly as possible with a solution to your problem. Incidentally, if you should develop an unusual or promising idea and would like assistance (or advice) with regard to it—write to me about that, too. I'll see that you get an answer.

Steven West
New York, New York
April 1977

CHAPTER ONE

THE ILLUSION
AND THE REALITY
OF SUCCESS

When I started to look into the lives of the richest men in the world—past and present—I thought I was going to find out what made them so *smart*. Instead, I came up with a lot of unexpected answers.

I discovered that the majority of the world's richest men—past and present—were not smarter than the average man; in fact, a lot of them were stupid.

Now I'm talking about the original millionaires and billionaires—not their offsprings; they're an even sorrier lot than the old man was.

The more I read, the more puzzled I became. If they weren't smarter than the people they grew up with; the people they competed with; the people they manipulated—then what was it they had that the others didn't have?

Was it just dumb luck? No. That wasn't it. They may have been stupid but not that stupid. Only a fool depends on luck to get what he wants out of life. Real gamblers don't gamble at all—they play sure things.

All right; so it wasn't brains and it wasn't luck. There had to be something—some simple common denominator that every one of these men had.

One thing they all had in common—they didn't start out rich—most of them were as poor as church mice. very few of them had a decent education.

Yet, all around them were 'better' people (by society's standards)—smarter people, better educated people; with all the required manners and social graces.

These 'better' people just stood and watched, without understanding, while the men and women who were destined to become the world's richest people, moved quietly and steadily past them.

The majority of 'better' (and less than better) people in this world still don't understand how these rare men and women achieved their phenomenal successes. It's still a mystery even though most of the 'rich' have told the simple, honest truth about how they did it.

Most of the people in this world do not believe that they have been given the simple, honest truth—mainly because it is simple. So simple that a child could do it. In fact, many of the richest men in the world first set their feet on the paths to riches as a child.

Aristotle Onassis began his rise to riches as a shoe shine boy in the streets of Athens. Andrew Carnegie started as a newspaper boy.

The simple fact that every rich man knew, instinctively, as a child, was that money was not something you spent—money was something that you used—over and over—but never spent it. They knew, quite early in life, that money was a tool; a means to an end rather than an end in itself. This is a critically important idea.

That was the first common denominator.

The next was the fact that each of them wanted one thing above all others—they wanted to be rich. They put everything else out of their minds; concentrated all of their efforts upon that one thing, and let nothing and no one interfere with their desire to be rich.

The third important factor was that they did not try to achieve their goal in one giant leap. They chose, instead, to give themselves smaller, easily obtained goals and built them into a series of simple achievements.

In other words they placed one small success on top of another small success and eventually went, step-by-step up the ladder to the final objective—the biggest success.

When I had extracted those three 'key' factors I was ready to start creating a blueprint that would enable me to do exactly what they had done—with one major difference.

I had no intention of devoting my life to becoming a millionaire—I just wanted to live like one now while I was still young enough to enjoy it.

My blueprint had to be different. I already had three important parts locked up but there were more parts needed. To get them would require a different viewpoint.

I began to study the millionaires that were alive and kicking all around me in today's society. What was there about them that was different? That was easy.

The rich looked rich. The wealthy men and women wore beautiful clothes; rode in very expensive cars; lived in beautiful homes; traveled by private jet planes; sailed on ocean-going yachts; wintered in luxurious and exclusive resorts and islands; were admired, envied, photographed and written about.

Another important part fell into place. Then another; and now I had the first, rough, experimental blueprint. Then, after a lot of trial and error—changes—experimenting—thinking and re-thinking (all of which could be a book in itself) I finally arrived at the plan; a plan that worked so beautifully that I had it all—every last bit of it—within a year and a half.

I mean I really had the whole ball of wax; the clothes, the world's finest cars, a beautiful home, private jets, luxurious vacations—everything.

It was everything I'd ever wanted. I really enjoyed myself. I was happier than I'd ever been in my life. The part that pleased me most was how easy it had been once I'd worked out the formula. And it was all legitimate—every bit of it was legal.

Then, late one afternoon, I thought, *"if it's this easy—why not go for broke? Why not go all the way and actually become a millionaire instead of just living like one?*

I realized that I could—and it wouldn't take me a lifetime to do it because I had already laid the ground work when I started to live like a millionaire.

I could use the same principles I had established in my original formula. The only difference would be that I would have to really go to work—and I mean work. There's no playing around when you set out to really become rich. You have to buckle down and keep you're mind on what you're doing every minute that you're awake—and you're awake a lot. You learn to live on less sleep—and you keep yourself in top physical condition—just like an athlete who's shooting for a berth on the Olympic Team; because you are in the Olympics when you set out to make a real million.

It wasn't easy. It took years—hard years—but I've made a lot more than the original million I was aiming at; and I intend to make a lot more before I retire because, as I said before, the 'money game' is the greatest game in the world and I love it.

If that's what you really want, then you buckle down and study this book because, when you've mastered the principles in this book, and learn how to live like a millionaire, you'll be half way to your goal because you will have completed your basic training in the art of becoming a member of the millionaire's club.

Just remember, when you're living like a millionaire it's all an illusion—not reality. The world will assume that you are a millionaire even though you're not, simply because you will look, dress, eat, drive, fly and vacation like a millionaire—so—obviously you must be one or you couldn't afford to do all those things.

The fact is you will be able to afford all those things because they will cost you next to nothing. I mean that. Sounds impossible? Not at all. You'll understand why, when we get down to brass tacks in later chapters.

What I am about to tell you now is the general idea of how and why the formula works. You will be given the full blueprint step-by-step in subsequent chapters. Just remember that this chapter only contains a general description of the overall plan. It is not the plan itself.

I'm telling you this so that you do not make the mistake of believing that once you have read this chapter you are ready to put the plan into action. You will not be ready. There is a lot of reading, preparation and a lot of practice before you are ready to put the plan into actual operation.

Just remember one thing and keep it firmly fixed in your mind. When you are given the total plan you must follow it to the letter. Do not attempt to tinker with it. You must think of it as a specific recipe for a certain kind of dessert. If you decide to change some of the ingredients or change the sequence of the steps to be taken the end result will be a mess instead of dessert.

It's exactly the same with the specific plan you will be given. Tinker with it—change any sequence of steps and you will have a mess on your hands.

All right. Here's the general idea. There are certain things that are absolutely necessary to this plan.

    (1)   You must have a steady job or a source of regular income. This is a vital necessity.

    (2)   You must have a 'stake'—a sum of money not less than $2,000.00 (Two Thousand Dollars) If you haven't got it

now, don't worry, I'll show you how you can save it, painlessly, out of your regular income. But it is necessary to the plan.

(3) You must be in reasonably good health. If you are not—if you're overweight—sickly—nervous—eating improperly—all that will have to change. Here again I will help you but you must make a determined effort to cooperate. Good health is vital to this plan.

(4) Your mental attitude will have to change. Your attitude towards yourself and others will have to be altered. I can help you. I have achieved it myself and I have helped thousands of people to achieve it through a book I wrote called "Mental Calisthenics". Again, you will have to cooperate.

Rest assured that your mental attitude will change, for the better. The odd part is that once you start to change it will become easier and easier because a healthier mental outlook is more enjoyable.

When you finally achieve your goal of living like a millionaire you're going to find that you have started to think like a millionaire. Then you will understand the basic difference between the way the rich think and the way the rest of the world thinks.

It's simply a matter of taking one step at a time until you reach your first limited objective. Then taking another series of steps to reach a slightly higher goal. Before you know it you have reached the ultimate goal.

It really isn't hard to do. It just takes patience and practice, practice, practice. The rewards are directly proportional to the effort you put into it. The more effort the greater your rewards and the quicker you receive them.

Your total investment (the two thousand dollars) will be returned to you a thousand fold. Actually you will never let go of it. It will be earning interest all the time you are using it. If that sounds impossible, trust me. You'll find that it's true.

Now, let's move on. We will assume that you have all the basic needs. You have a steady job or source of income. You have your $2,000.00 stake. Your health is excellent and your mental outlook is healthy.

Our next step is to give you an additional identity as a real professional. We will show you, later on, exactly how you can acquire a legitimate and legal identity as the top executive of your own corporation.

We will assume that this has happened and that you now have a professional office, business cards and stationery; a business telephone and listing.

Our next step will be to prepare you to physically emerge in your new identity. This will require that you are properly groomed. From the top of your head to the tips of your toes you will have to look the part you are about to play in real life.

Make no mistake about it—you are going to play a part just as if you were on the stage. The difference will be that your stage will be life itself.

You can do it. You have been playing a part since the first day you entered social life. When you entered kindergarten you began to play a part. You told everyone who you were when you gave them your name but you did more—you told them who you were by the way you acted without being aware that you were doing it.

The part we are going to prepare you for is different than the role you are playing now. You are going to play the part of a successful, top executive on the way to becoming a millionaire.

It won't be as difficult as you might think. You see, by the time you're ready, you will not only look the part but you'll feel it as well. People will accept you in this new role because they will have no reason not to.

After you have played the part for awhile you will actually become the part you're playing. You will be a chief executive rapidly rising to success. You will, by that time have developed an aura of power and success. You will actually possess that rare and powerful mantle called charisma. People will respond to you as though they were hypnotized and, to a certain degree, they will be.

People—all people—are dazzled by success. They gravitate to successful people because they want to bask in the light of your success—they enjoy being seen with successful people because, subconsciously, they feel that some of it may rub off on them. They yearn to be successful, but that's all they do—just yearn.

You will be living your success.

Just remember—the role you will be playing requires constant practice. Unlike the stage you will not remove the greasepaint at the end of the performance *because there is no end to the performance.* You will be on all the time. The show goes on twenty four hours a day. You never step out of your role—not for an instant.

It really isn't difficult. You'll actually enjoy playing the part. You won't be stiff in it either. You will find that you are more relaxed than you have ever been in your entire life thanks to the exercises we are going to give you. You will also be more aware than you have ever been before—and something else will happen—something astonishing. You will begin to see into people with a depth of understanding that will amaze you.

People will be aware of this ability and it will raise you to a higher level in their eyes. They will begin to endow you with much more power than you actually have.

Then, oddly enough, as you sense this attitude of people towards you, you will begin to gain that power. You will begin to sense your own developing charisma and realize that illusion can actually become reality; that you can become the part you were playing.

As you begin to relax and enjoy the role and realize that, with each passing day, it is becoming a reality—another strange thing will happen. You will become gentler and softer spoken because real power is soft spoken—it proclaims itself—you do not have to speak for it. In fact—the very act of speaking softly and being gentle with people enhances the aspect of power—makes it more visible to people.

Only braggarts and cowards speak harshly and try to bully people. They're trying to convince themselves as well as other people that they are really important.

The really important people—the really powerful people—the really rich people—have no need to try to impress people. They are impressive mainly because they are so relaxed—so gentle—so friendly and helpful to anyone. Why not? The powerful are not afraid of anything on this Earth.

I can guarantee that if you practice your part every day—it won't be long before you are the part you play.

Now—what about money? Actually—aside from your 'stake' (which we will show you how to get) you will find that legitimate credit is one of the easiest things to get in our society if you don't seem to need it.

I mean that if you appear to be a top executive of a corporation who is rising to success, then the financial world assumes that you intend to use money as a tool—rather than just to spend it on luxuries.

You see the rich don't spend money—they use it to make more money. That's the name of the game. That's why the rich get richer and the poor get poorer.

The poor have to spend what little they have. The rich never spend their own money—they spend other people's money.

Let's take an example of the difference between someone who spends money and someone who uses money. We'll use two women for our example since women still have a tougher time getting credit than men do. We have two women—Joan and Alice. They both work in similar jobs—both earn the same amount of money. Both of them need a car. Joan arranges for a car loan at her local bank. That's not too hard because there is collateral (the car) and Joan puts down a third in cash. Her new car costs her $120.00 per month. She's paying about 18% (actually) per year for the loan. It's a little tight but she'll have the car paid off in three years.

Joan figures that she can make it if she just puts $30.00 a week away and—well, she needs the car and who cares? Joan is a fool. She's not only spent the cash for the down payment— she's also put herself in hock for three years and because of the finance charges she's spent a hell of a lot more for the car than she realizes.

Alice is something else. Alice is a woman who uses money. She knew she was going to need a new car so she just kept putting money in the bank (a savings bank where the interest was highest) for three years. At the end of the three years Alice had accumulated about $5,000.00. Did she take the money out and buy the car for cash? Not Alice. She took out a passbook loan for $4,000.00 and bought the best new car—at the best price (the leftover models at the end of the year) for cash.

She kept on putting her $30.00 a week in the bank—paying off the passbook loan. That loan incidentally only cost her 2½% (which was the difference between the interest the bank was paying her on her deposited $5,000.00 and the cost of the passbook loan (about 8%).

Now as she kept paying off that loan, her actual cost of the loan was being reduced. Also Alice was under no compulsion to pay back the loan—she could pay it off as fast or as slowly as she wanted to.

Let's suppose that Alice pays off her loan to herself at the same rate that Joan pays off her loan to the bank. At the end of three years Alice has her original $5,000.00 (plus interest) and her 3 year old car. Joan doesn't have a dime—just her old car.

There is a third alternative that should be mentioned. Either of them could have leased a car. There are all kinds of lease arrangements. In some cases you can lease virtually any car on the market with no down payment and just the first month's rental plus a month for security. You can also arrange for insurance and maintenance to be included in your lease. An obvious advantage to leasing is the 100% tax write-off you can take if the car is used solely for business purposes.

The point is, whatever you do, think before you spend money and try to find a way to use it, instead. Never spend your capital—use it as collateral.

Aristotle Onassis built his fortune on that principle of never spending capital.

Once you actually embark upon your program you'll learn how to stop spending money and start using it to make money.

Incidentally, the reason why you have to have a steady income or a steady job, is simply because there will be a period of time without income while you are building your new image.

You will use that stake as seed money—and we will show you how to make it expand into a small fortune.

Now—let's see where you are right now in our general

scheme. You are the established top executive in a legal corporation. You are well groomed—you are developing poise and charisma—now you need some extra equipment.

You are ready to take the first outside step in your new career. You already have saved up your stake—your $2,000.00—you are now ready to go.

You take that 'stake' to a savings bank—open a savings account for the entire amount—then take a passbook loan for $1,500.00 The cost for this amount for an entire year is about $37.50 in interest. You are under no pressing obligation to pay it off. You need only pay back the interest (if you don't they will withdraw it from your deposited capital). You are going to pay it back however—using the same method that you employed to get your stake—putting a certain amount away each week. The only difference is that you will place half that amount towards reducing your loan and half in depositing to your account.

Now you have $1,500.00 of the bank's money to start using for things you will need. Your next step will be to pick out five banks in the community you intend to operate in. At the first bank you will ask to see the bank manager. You will introduce yourself (with your business card, give him your corporate papers and open a business account. You will say very little to him—rather you will press him to speak to you. You will ask him questions about the services the bank offers. Let him trot out his wares. You will be cordial and friendly but slightly reserved. Your deposit of $1,500.00 will speak for you. As you listen to him you will note (if he has perception) that he is sizing you up. He is looking at your clothes—your hands—your hair—and is trying to form an opinion. He knows from your card and corporate papers that you are a top executive. He is impressed with your bona fides and with your appearance. You look like a winner to him—and he wants winners because that's the name of his game. He needs successful people. He needs new companies who will do business with his bank. He also wants business loans, too. He will—if he's impressed with you—arrange to open a line of credit if you let him—do not let him do it. It would require a financial statement. You're not

ready for that yet. He's certain to offer you his business card—
if he doesn't—ask for it. You'll need everyone's business card,
eventually.

When your business is concluded—leave—do not dawdle—
do not engage in idle conversation. If he attempts to do so—
look at your watch—smile pleasantly and tell him that you
have an engagement and leave briskly because time is money.

You will not visit the next four banks until your new printed
checks arrive (because you'll be reusing the same money) so
your next stop is the local real estate office. There you will
again introduce yourself and announce that you have two
needs. One is information about the availability of office
space—the other is the availability of a suitable small estate—
one that could be employed both for social gatherings as well as
business seminars and special business meetings.

Remember that you are 'on stage' with this real estate agent.
Be relaxed, friendly and confident. You are only asking for
information. If the agent offers to take you to some locations—
make an appointment for another time—again, the impression
you must give is that while you are relaxed and friendly—time
is money and you are busy and have important engagements.
You cannot afford—at the moment—to spend time being
driven around by a real estate agent. Again—when your
business is concluded—leave briskly—do not dawdle or
engage in idle conversation.

A note here about your car. If it is not a decent looking car
do not park in front of the bank or the real estate office. People
will judge you quicker by the car you drive than the clothes you
wear. You can wear blue jeans and step out of a Rolls and get
away with it but you cannot be dressed beautifully and step out
of a beat up old car. It won't wash.

Park the car a distance away and walk.

We'll put you in a decent car later on and then you can drive
up to any meeting.

Your next stop is at the local photographers. Introduce
yourself with your business card; ask about costs for single,
executive portraits as well as group pictures. Find out what the
charges are for 'location picture shooting'; how much time is
required between the time the pictures are taken and you
receive your finished prints. Get the full story.

Here again you are out to make the proper kind of an impression. You may be certain that the photographer as well as the real estate agent and the bank manager will be talking about you before the day is out. If you create a successful aura of confidence there is no doubt as to how you will be discussed.

When your business is concluded—leave briskly. Do not enter into idle conversation. Listen carefully to the answers to your questions write down the pertinent information—obtain a business card from the photographer and then leave.

Your next stop is the local newspaper. Obtain, from the girl at the desk, the name of the business editor—the publisher—the local news editor. Do not attempt to gain audience with any of them at this time. If the girl (or woman) at the desk should ask for your name—give her your business card. Remember that you are on stage there, too. This is another person who will add to the picture of you that will be formed.

Stop at the local newsstand and pick up all the available local weekly and daily newspapers. They will provide you with one of the sources for the list you will assemble of publicity sources, as well as a prospect list.

Your telephone book (yellow pages) will give you a list of all the newspapers (and business papers) that serve your particularly area. The yellow pages also list new car dealers, doctors, lawyer and other professional people who will be your future prospects. There is another excellent source for prospects which you can obtain from the research librarian at your local library. It's the Dun & Bradstreet Directories of million and half-million dollar companies and corporations.

Your next project is publicity. We'll touch on that subject briefly here, because it's fully covered in Chapter Seven (How To Use Publicity and Public Relations). The point here is, whenever you set up a publicity release (on your own stationery or on special Press Release stationery) be sure to use a decent typewriter with clean keys. If you haven't got a decent typewriter then take it to a public stenographer who will type it on an electric IBM or a special 'repro' machine. This typed publicity release will be your camera-ready mechanical.

When you take this 'master' to a printer who offers 'instant' printing, he will probably print 100 copies for about $5.00. He also can print up your corporate announcements (which are mailed directly to the top people in the business community). The corporate announcements which usually consist of matching baronial cards and envelopes should cost about $20.00 per hundred.

Photography is another requirement. You will need pictures of yourself, your associates, offices, business building, etc.

If you're going to operate in a small community then make a personal call. If not, call for prices on the telephone. There are a number of firms in or near every city which specialize in making prints of your original pictures at very low cost. When you order, a good rule of thumb is to order three times the number of prints relative to the number of news sources. For example, if you intend to mail your release to 50 newspapers, buy 150 prints. The reason is simply that you should send releases to the managing editor, the local news editor and the business news editor. One of them may decide to run just the picture and caption. Another may run the entire publicity release. The third may do nothing.

By sending to all three men you increase your chances of getting into print, and—at the same time—your publicity release has been seen by three important people. All three of them can be important to you in the future. Not just for publicity purposes but also because these three men are key figures in the community you are attempting to influence.

You'll need captions for any pictures you send to a newspaper because a picture can (and does) become separated from your news release. When it does it becomes meaningless unless there is a caption affixed to it which (in a brief paragraph) tells the story.

Captions are simple to write. Just remember the three W's (Who, Why, Where?) Here are some examples:

1. ONE PERSON PHOTO

John J. Jones, president of UVISCO, a corporate leasing firm, has announced the opening of new executive offices at the Blankman Building, 350 Broadway Avenue, Dawson City.

2. MORE THAN ONE PERSON

John J. Jones (R) president of UVISCO, welcomes
attorney Harold Doe (L) and tax expert Phillip Hoe
(C) as affiliates of the corporate leasing firm during
the formal opening of UVISCO's new executive
offices in the Blankman Building, 350 Broadway,
Dawson City.

Here's a simple way to cut the cost of printing your picture
captions. Once you have decided on the text of your picture
caption, type it cleanly, four times (one under another) on a
blank sheet of 8½ x 11 white bond. Be sure to leave sufficient
space between each, repeated caption. Take this 'master' to
your printer have him print 75 copies. When you cut them
apart you will have 300 picture captions. Affix the picture
captions to the pictures so that the text appears at the bottom
of the picture. Use scotch tape on the back of the picture to
secure the caption. Never tape on the front of the picture
because you'll ruin it.

A professional looking publicity release will have a better
chance of being printed and, it adds to your growing image.
Some of your publicity releases will always be printed. You can
improve the chance of being printed by making certain that
your publicity release contains 'news'. We'll show you how to
'make' news in the chapter on publicity and public relations.

Now, if you've planned it right, your publicity release should
be appearing in the newspapers at the same time your
corporate announcement is arriving on the desks of the leading
executives in your business community.

You should, by now have gained both insight and
understanding of the general plan of this book. In short, you
are aware of the basic needs:

1. You must have a steady income
2. You need a stake of about $2,000.00
3. A correct mental attitude is a must
4. Your physical health is important
5. You must be prepared to play a 'role'

You have, in this chapter, been given some indication of how
you will conduct yourself in various situations. You have been
shown how to establish a bank relationship and gain valuable
publicity. You have been given a brief idea of how to create a
new 'image'. This is just the beginning.

In the chapters that follow you will learn, step by step, how easy it is to obtain all of the image enhancers—the visible symbols of success—the luxury cars—the corporate limousine—the expensive wardrobe—the fully furnished corporate offices—the luxury apartment—the millionaire's mansion—the worldwide traveling to exclusive playgrounds of the rich and powerful.

Just keep in mind, at all times, that while you are fully aware that what you have created is the illusion of a millionaire's life—to everyone else it will be real.

They will only be able to see the outward trappings and, as you continue to practice and perfect your part as a successful top executive well on his way to millions, you will be getting closer to actually becoming one.

In the next chapter we are going to discuss the various aspects of a new full or part-time career you will need to fit yourself into. We're going to discuss a number of different careers, and you must select the one you will feel most comfortable in. That's vitally important because you must be comfortable with this new career if you are to succeed in playing the role—and certainly if you are going to make it an actual career.

A word here about education. It is not important that you have a college degree—we can show you how to obtain a perfectly valid one from an accredited college or university but—I repeat—it is not important.

What is important is that you become well informed and well read. You must begin to read at least two newspapers right at the outset—one is the Wall Street Journal, which is one of the most informative and easiest reading papers in the world. The other paper is your region's daily newspaper because you have to keep up with your community news. The local weekly is another good choice for local news.

Something else you must start practicing is public speaking because you are going to speak at local service clubs like the Rotary—the Lions, etc. Oh yes you are! It's important for you to be seen and heard by the people in the business community. Don't worry—we'll help you with that part of it too.

The one thing that should sustain you through all of the effort you're going to make is the fun aspect of what you're doing. You're going to enjoy becoming a real celebrity—and you will be. You're going to enjoy the benefits that go with it.

There's work ahead of you—this book can do a great deal to help you achieve your goal but you have to help—you will have to buckle down and do some of the work but it won't be hard work—it will be fun work.

I think, before we close this chapter, that I should leave you with a thought to remember and do something about. That's the way you run your personal life right now. It's safe to bet that you don't run it like a business.

Well you are going to have to start running it like a business. We'll tell you exactly how in the chapter on Finances. But meanwhile you can make a note to get an expense account book in your local stationery store.

Starting tomorrow you will write down everything you spend money on. Just write it down without trying to change anything just yet. Write down everything—food—candy—movies—dinners out—newspapers—cigarettes—liquor—clothing—everything.

We'll talk about it later on. Just start doing that now.

I would suggest, at this point, that you take a break. As I pointed out to you, in the beginning, this book is not designed to be read at a single sitting. There's a lot to absorb; a lot of new ideas and concepts. Take time to think about them and become comfortable with them.

The main thing to remember is the fact that you now know that it is possible to create a brand new image of yourself; a success image that will eventually make it possible for you to live like a millionaire.

After you have taken your break (and a short walk) sit down and re-read this entire chapter. Take particular note of those places you marked. Are those points clear to you now? Do you understand them? They should be, but if they're not—then jot down the page number and the paragraph in question. Keep doing this as you read the rest of the book. When you've finished reading the book, check all your notes. If the questions are still unanswered and the points still not understood, drop the notes in the mail to me, care of my publishers. I'll write back as quickly as I can.

Meanwhile put the book away. Your mind, while you're sleeping tonight, will sort out all this new material for you.

CHAPTER TWO

YOUR
SECOND CAREER

This is your first specific step towards a full understanding of what you must do to reach your primary goal of living like a millionaire on an ordinary income.

We are going to explore all of the facets of your new 'second' career. Now, unless you have a steady source of income that permits you to work full time at this 'second' career, you will have to work at it part time. Please keep this in mind when you reach that moment when you have to make you decision as to which career you will choose.

I would suggest that you limit your choice of a second career to just two types of businesses.

1. The kind of business that provides expert advice and counselling to clients.
2. The kind of business that permits you to act as a 'middle man' or DISTRIBUTOR who obtains products for a client.

The reasons for this should be fairly obvious. A service business requires little or no overhead in comparison to business that produces a physical product. There is no need to invest in raw material; no need for converting equipment; no need for packaging, excessive shipping, warehousing, inventory and the like.

You will, therefore, limit your 'service' to that of a 'consultant' or a distributor. In the first instance you will supply clients with 'advice and counsel'; in the second instance you will obtain goods and service on behalf of your client. You may also, as we shall explain later, act as a referral agency.

The main point is that the career you choose should enable you to carry the total operating 'equipment' of your business in your head, on your back and in your handsome attache case.

This means that your 'overhead' will be practically zero and thus your 'profits' can be quite large relatively speaking. It also means that your chances for success are considerably enhanced.

Now let's take the question of a career 'fit' which is one of the most important considerations from the standpoint of credibility. You cannot simply throw a dart into a group of possible careers and assume that you can make a success of it regardless of which one the dart struck. It has to be a career that 'fits' your ability to handle it so that prospective clients and the general public will believe that you have this capability.

The simplest way to arrive at some understanding of your capabilities is to take a piece of paper and begin listing all of the skills, hobbies, inclinations or any unique talents you might possess.

Start at the top of the page with the job you now have. Describe it. Is there anything that you are now doing that could be turned into a 'service' business? Think about what you are being paid to do for your employer. You must know your job very well. Is there any aspect of it—or any connecting activity with which you are thoroughly familiar that could be turned into a service that you could sell to a number of other firms?

Are there vendors supplying services to your employers? Could you supply those services if you had your own company?

Now think about your circle of friends. Do any of them supply a service to different companies? Do you know anything about the kinds of services they supply? Do you think you could supply those kinds of services? Would you be interested in doing it? That's a most important consideration with regard to your choice of 'second' career. It should be some thing you would enjoy doing.

Do you have any hobbies? I recall the way a close friend turned his hobby into a service business and, in addition to becoming an 'authority' on the subject he also made considerable profit. He collected coins for quite a few years and recently, when the dramatic upturn came in coin values (particularly gold coins) he made a substantial profit. He used the windfall as a 'stake' to start his now extensive coin distributor business.

He gave a number of highly interesting 'talks' as part of the programs of service clubs like the Rotary, Lions, and Kiwanis Clubs. The end result of those talks was a steady influx of businessmen, with money to invest, who obtained his services as a coin 'broker'.

So you see, a hobby can be turned into a profitable and enjoyable 'second' career.

Do you have a 'talent' that you are not using now in your present job? Perhaps it can be turned into a 'service' business.

Are you a 'whiz' with figures? Do you enjoy bookkeeping or accounting? That ability could be turned to excellent advantage in many different areas of financial counseling or actual 'services'.

How far have you progressed with your listings on that separate piece of paper? If there aren't too many skills, hobbies or talents listed perhaps you should write down the kinds of things you would 'like' to do if you had the background and ability. These can be achieved.

Let's take a look at some career 'choices' and perhaps one of them might strike your fancy. One of the easiest 'skills' to acquire (if you like figures) is the title of a
TAX CONSULTANT.

Virtually any reasonably intelligent man or woman who feels at ease with basic mathematics can become a Tax Consultant in a relatively short time. In fact there are companies that will train you—and then hire you—to do Income Tax work during the peak periods.

With that background under your belt it would be a relatively simple thing to set up a corporation and go into business for yourself on an all-year-round basis. If you offered your services at a modest fee, you could easily form a pool of small business firms as your client foundation. You could handle their tax problems on a monthly, quarterly or semi-annual basis. Once you had established yourself you would be in a strong position with regard to 'counseling' as well as direct services.

In a later chapter we will show you how to turn that counseling aspect into a tool which will enable you to acquire many of the 'visible symbols of success' with little or no cash investment.

Do you have a natural bent for
INTERIOR DECORATION?

Then you have a perfect basis for a 'service' business. The 'broker' concept works almost totally in Interior Decoration services. You also act as a counselor, so that you are really covering almost the total spectrum of services.

As a 'broker' you are responsible for seeking, finding, purchasing (with your client's money) the drapes, fixtures and furniture for a single room or an entire home. Some decorators concentrate on hotels, motels or office buildings. Others are content with individual homes or apartments.

You will, in the course of business, have many opportunities to meet and become friendly with executives in many of the firms you will do business with on behalf of your clients. Companies that manufacture paint, wall paper, floorcoverings, mirrors, lamps, furniture, drapes, plumbing fixtures, sinks and bathtubs are just some of the firms that you will be dealing with. You will also work, at times with architects and real estate developers. The business contacts you will make are widespread and will, again, as we pointed out before, offer you opportunities to acquire your 'visible symbols of success' with little or no investment. We will advise you on this 'art' later on.

Obviously, just having an inclination towards Interior Decoration will not be sufficient for you to set yourself up as either a practioner or a consultant. You will have to take some courses (which are readily available in the schools or colleges near you. These can be either credit or non-credit courses and are relatively inexpensive). You can also avail yourself of the wealth of material that is on hand at your public library.

You can contact an interior decorating firm and make an appointment to visit their offices where, you may question them as to the extent of their services, methods of payments, fees and other data.

If you think you would enjoy doing this kind of work, you could, with a little application, become proficient enough to actually engage in this activity.

Remember that even though we are in the process of creating an illusion you must be thoroughly acquainted with whatever profession you choose as your 'second' career. You may never actually obtain a client or a contract but you should be competent enough to carry out an assignment if you should be given one.

The title of INVESTMENT COUNSELOR seems, at first glance to be a weighty one. It conjures up visions of the men who counsel the rich or the newly rich, as to all the mysterious ways of investing money to secure the best 'return'—the best income and so forth.

If this sort of thing appeals to you, then by all means give this form of service careful consideration. Oddly enough, virtually anyone with a 'clean' credit rating and an honest legal background (no criminal convictions) can receive official accreditation from the Securities Exchange Commission merely upon application.

However, simply by becoming an 'accredited' investment counselor, you cannot simply go into business and expect to achieve any degree of credibility without taking the time and trouble to become thoroughly familiar with this particular field. At the very least you will have to become familiar with the 'language' of investment. There is a wealth of written material available to you at your library.

Your commercial banks not only supply material but have investment specialists on hand to advise and counsel you; most major stockbrokers will send you material or be happy to sit down with you and discuss ways and means of investing your capital.

With a little effort and some heavy reading you can become knowledgeable enough to pass for a real investment counselor and might even, on occasion, offer sound advice.

Your main concern is to be able to discuss your profession intelligently and convincingly. With luck and care you may even acquire some clients and thus add further credibility to your 'image'.

How does the title EDUCATIONAL MATERIALS CONSULTANT strike you? Do you have any opinions about the kinds of toys children should be given? Do you enjoy reading? Have you ever wondered about the people who write and produce children's books? How much do you know about things like 'language labs,' talking typewriters—sectional 'break-away' objects—textbook requirements and contracts—audio/visual equipment—the list is endless because the business of education is BIG business. It runs into billions of dollars a year. It's also a fascinating business.

Here again, if you want to become known as the top executive of an Educational Materials Consulting Corporation you have to do your homework.

There are schools to visit; companies to contact who will send you material in the form of brochures and catalogs.

In the matter of schools, it is a simple matter to discover the person responsible for the purchase of educational material. Arrange to meet him—you can tell him that you're a writer doing an article on the art of purchasing educational materials and he'll probably invite you to lunch. Take along a notebook and let him tell you how smart he is and what he has to know in order to make judicial purchases. He'll give you enough material to fill two notebooks and be very grateful for the opportunity. Learn to listen attentively. You'll get a mountain of knowledge that way. You could be a VENTURE CAPITAL SPECIALIST. There's an exciting concept. It sounds impressive but in the final analysis it's just a 'broker' who happens to deal in money rather than a product. There are people with a 'plan' or an idea for an invention—or possibly an idea for a new kind of company. They need money (venture capital). Then there are companies, or people with money to invest. They're looking for companies or inventions to invest in. The Venture Capital Specialist brings them together and collects a 'finders' fee.

The two ingredients for success are peculiar. The first ingredient—the companies or people that are looking for money are extremely easy to find. You just have to advertise and your mailbox will be choked in no time.

The second ingredient—finding people and companies with money to invest—is more difficult. They tend to keep a low profile, which is understandable. People and companies with money who are highly visible are bombarded with mail requests—just as you will be once you begin to advertise.

If you feel that this is the type of business you would enjoy, by all means try it. Just remember that you'll have plenty of homework in preparing for it.

One of the most useful tools you can obtain for this type of work is the excellent publication by Stanley M. Rubel— GUIDE TO VENTURE CAPITAL SOURCES. It's published by Capital Publishing Corporation, 10 South LaSalle Street, Chicago, Illinois 60603. It costs $47.50 but it's well worth it.

With this book in hand you can locate almost every reliable venture capital firm in the nation. The listings give the name and address of each firm; the names and titles of the officers of the company; the names of the people to contact; and the particular ventures they are interested in for investment purposes, and the limit of the amounts of money they have for investment.

If you don't want to spend the money for this book then visit the main branch of your library and ask the research librarian if she will let your xerox the library copy of the book. Each copy will run about 15¢ and you need only copy the pages with the firms that are closest to your geographical location.

The research librarian can order a copy of the book from the State Library Association if they don't have a copy on hand when you call.

The library can also help you dig out all the articles that have been written about venture capital in various magazines. That can furnish you with a broad education in the field at little or no expense other than the xerox costs for copying.

As to the matter of finding people and companies with money to invest, the trick is to let them find you. If your publicity and public relations campaign is successful, you may be sure that you will begin to receive inquiries from highly paid professionals like lawyers, doctors, dentists and morticians. They are constantly looking for good investments.

PUBLIC RELATIONS COUNSELOR. That has a nice round ring to it. If you think you might like to become the top executive in that kind of a professional practice, then you'd better gain some understanding of the field. There are two aspects to Public Relations. One is purely physical—that is the actual writing and producing of articles—mounting a special campaign—arranging for press conferences—creating special 'press kits' for dissemination to reporters and writers from magazines, newspapers and television stations. Arranging for interviews on talk shows—placing client products on game shows—a host of activities.

The other aspect is counseling. This is a highly specialized activity which requires a fine sense of what the end result will be of a certain kind of conduct on the part of the executive and/or the corporation.

Counseling covers the internal aspects of a corporation with regard to employee-relations and/or labor-relations. In a publicly held corporation there is the art of stockholder relations as well as the vital public relations with regard to investment firms as well as investment reporters.

In short, public relations counseling is the fine art of guiding the activities of executives and/or corporations towards the goal of image enhancement rather than towards deterioration.

Here again, homework is in order. There is plenty of reading material available at your local library. There are also courses available in public relations on a credit or non-credit basis at your local college or university.

There are some public relations firms that are politically oriented. You might also be tempted to enter the P.R. field on a 'local' political level. Do not do it. You will find it more judicious to remain above the political arena because you can only be on one side or the other. That means you are an 'enemy' to the other side. You want to be friends with the world.

This doesn't mean that when you become proficient in your field that you cannot 'privately' counsel a friend entering politics—with the clear understanding that it is not to be made public. If your friend should win his post then you have a 'friend at court' so to speak.

How would you like to be the president of a NATIONAL DISTRIBUTING CORPORATION? You could be in actual operation, within a period of a few weeks, with a fully functioning company that could make money for you. It's not very difficult to do and requires very little money to get started; less than $200.00 would be all you'd need for your initial capital.

There are hundreds of legitimate companies that would be happy to set you up as an authorized distributor of their products. In many cases they will give you a defined territory, supply you with product sample kits, printed invoices, letterheads and catalogs.

There is no need to stock the products, just send in the orders and they will send you the products. In many cases they will 'drop ship' for you—that is, send the products directly to your customer—sometimes with your company label affixed.

It can be a fascinating (as well as profitable) second career for you. Naturally as president of the corporation you can gain a lot of valuable publicity at little or no cost. (See Chapter on publicity and public relations for details.)

There are several excellent magazines that offer you in-depth articles on starting your own business, raising capital, and give shrewd advice relative to mail order ventures, getting into franchised distributions and direct selling. Here are the names and addresses:

FREE ENTERPRISE
The Capitalistic Reporter
800 Second Avenue
New York, N.Y. 10017

SPECIALTY SALESMEN
 AND BUSINESS
 OPPORTUNITIES
Communication Channels, Inc.
307 N. Michigan Avenue
Chicago, Illinois 60601

SALESMAN'S
 OPPORTUNITY
John Hancock Center
Suite 1460
875 N. Michigan Avenue
Chicago, Illinois 60611

INCOME
 OPPORTUNITIES
David Publications
229 Park Avenue South
New York, N.Y. 10003

When you write to these publishing companies, enclose a check for $1.00 and ask for a sample copy of the particular magazine you want. They'll probably send you the copy of the magazine plus subscription information and might even mail back your check. If not—it's worth more than a dollar to you, because those magazines will give you valuable information.

A variation of the National Distribution Corporation is a National Mail Order business. If you can locate interesting, unique and highly saleable items, there is a good chance that you can sell them profitably through the mail. You will need capital for advertising of course, but there is one way to advertise without spending a fortune up front.

A friend of mine developed a highly effective program on How To Stop Smoking. After carefully analyzing the various methods of advertising—in terms of CPM (cost per thousand) which is simply a way of calculating the actual cost of reaching 1,000 people with one ad. For example, if a magazine had a circulation of 100,000 subscribers and charged $100.00 for a small ad, the CPM would be $1.00 per thousand people. . . . he decided that readership ads in national publications would give him the greatest return at the lowest cost.

However there was still a considerable sum of money which would have to be allocated for the advertising budget. He managed to overcome that obstacle by creating a new company as a division of his corporation called Aardvark Advertising (not the real name) and had good looking letterheads and envelopes printed up.

Then he sent letters to 20 different publications requesting media kits, rate cards and advance notice of the editorial contents of the magazines. He also announced that his agency had recently become agency of record for several new clients and listed his own corporations.

When he received the kits, he sent back reservation orders with copies of the ads to be inserted. 16 of the 20 publications accepted the ads but 4 publications asked for a check with order.

Now the interesting part was that some publications had a deadline of two weeks prior to publication and others had a 4 week PTP (prior to publication) deadline. When the ads broke and the money began pouring in from around the country, my friend paid the 4 week PTP publications first and the 2 week PTP later.

His agency made 15% commission on the total dollars spent (and gained an excellent credit rating) and he wound up with a multi-million dollar mail order business within two years.

His total investment was intelligence, keen imagination and a few dollars for stationery.

A word of warning here. Do not set up your own corporation until you have thoroughly studied your new profession and until you have gained some practical experience with it. You must be completely satisfied with this new career or you will not be happy in it. That happiness is one of the most important 'keys' to your ultimate success.

You must enjoy engaging in this new career. You must enjoy your new prestige and the new respect you will command as you practice it. You will understand the significance of that when you read the chapter on 'mental preparation'.

Now, while you are studying your new profession you should also be investigating 'target' markets for your services. You want to discover the 'key' people in the companies within that 'target' market because you will begin to mount a campaign to make them aware that you and your company exist.

This will require letter writing as well as the use of publicity and public relations (Chapter Seven) and so you had better become proficient at letter writing too.

Just remember that whatever profession you choose you must be able to discuss it intelligently. That means you must become mind-saturated with information about your particular profession. That's easy to do if you become proficient in 'screening' everything you see or hear by asking yourself the questions:

"What effect will that have on my profession? Is that a good or bad thing? How will other people react to this news with regard to my profession?

These are exactly the questions you would ask yourself if you really were the professional you are trying to become. The odd part is the fact that by thinking, in this manner, you will shortly become that professional.

Just as people who continually think success become successful; people who think professionally actually become professionals in fact.

The essence of the material covered in this chapter is the fact that it is possible to enter a new, prestigious and exciting career instantly. There is no need to resign yourself to a lifetime of boring, repetitive, sub-standard jobs when you now realize that a top-level position in an exciting new profession is within easy reach. With just a little imagination and courage you can have a new 'second' career right now!

In our next chapter we're going to discuss the 'visible symbols' of success and show you how you can get them.

CHAPTER THREE

THE
VISIBLE SYMBOLS
OF SUCCESS
BASIC
and ADVANCED

Let's define the visible symbols of success so there is no misunderstanding about them. As I said, in the beginning of this book: the rich look rich.

The wealthy and successful men and women of this world wear beautiful clothes; ride in expensive cars; provide chauffeured limousine service for their clients and friends; fly in private aircraft, eat in the best restaurants where they are treated with the same deference shown to royalty. They also have magnificent offices with beautiful secretaries as well as luxurious homes in which they entertain royally.

Wealthy women are usually accompanied by very handsome, exquisitely groomed men. Wealthy men are usually accompanied by beautiful, exquisitely groomed women. Why not? They can afford it.

Now if you could enjoy all of the advantages I've just described then you would have all of the visible symbols of success. You would, in other words be living like a millionaire on an ordinary income.

You can do exactly that without doing anything that can be considered dishonest by you or anyone else.

I told you that everything in this book is legitimate and legal. The plan I am about to present is both. This plan, incidentally, may differ from the one described in the first chapter because this is a specific plan rather than a general plan. You may consider the other as theory and this as 'laboratory tested'.

I will presume that you have the basic requirements, meaning a steady job or a steady source of income and, that you have your original 'stake' of $2,000.00 to start with. You are also in reasonably good health and your mental attitude is correct and 'on course'. And you've chosen a 'second career'.

Let's begin with opening a savings account with your $2,000.00 stake. You then take a passbook loan for $1,500. which means you have 'capital' to use—you do not have any pressure in paying ·back the loan which—as I have already explained—is the simplest, fastest and cheapest way to borrow money. It actually costs you about $37.50 for the year if you don't pay a cent for an entire year. That's about 2½% per year which you must admit is cheap.

Your next stop is a commercial bank. You should ask to see the man in charge (bank manager) because you will always deal with the 'top' man, if possible. You must also be prepared to deal with the 'top' woman because more and more banks are elevating women to top executive positions.

A word of caution here. If you are a man and will be dealing with a woman executive do not attempt to charm her. Women executives are tough cookies. They didn't get to the top by being feminine—they got there by being smart, tough and exceptionally intuitive. Be thoroughly prepared with your story—rehearse it until you are letter perfect. And when you deliver it—deliver it exactly the way you would deliver it to a man. In other words—straight person-to-person. Let your inner strength and relaxation speak for you. Your story is extremely simple (keep it that way!)

You explain that although all you want to do at the moment is open a personal checking account, you wanted to meet her because you will, in the near future, be opening a corporate account. You wanted to deal directly with her in all financial matters pertaining to that account because you wanted to be certain that discretion with regard to the confidential nature of corporate activities would be exercised which might not be the case if you dealt with lower echelon people (and that's perfectly true).

If she makes any comments—listen—study her carefully—be pleasant but don't respond beyond politeness. Give the impression of relaxed reserve. Look directly at her eyes whether she is speaking to you or you are speaking to her.

Conclude your business—take your temporary checks and leave. Incidentally—deposit $1,000.00 as your opening deposit. Keep the other $500. as a reserve.

If you are a woman engaged in putting this plan into operation the same note of caution exists whether you are dealing with a man or a woman bank manager. Play it pleasant, relaxed and straight. Do not try to sell yourself. Let your inner power speak for you. You know who you are, you're a top executive on your way to your first million. Let the bank manager charm you.

Your story is exactly the same as outlined.

You will need professionally printed business cards for the next step in your operation. The best kind to order are the thermographed (raised letter) printing which gives the impression of engraving. They're not expensive and they do impress people much more than flat printed cards. The cost is approximately $10.00 for 250 business cards. They will probably take at least a week because very few printers have thermography equipment and usually farm out this type of business card.

The question is: What address will you put on the business card? You could use your home address but it would be more advantageous, in the beginning, to use an out-of-town address. There are a number of companies, around the nation, which will, for a modest fee, permit you to use their address and phone number for your 'company headquarters'.

You can find these companies in the following national newspapers. Usually on your local newsstands. If not, write to:

NATIONAL INQUIRER
600 South East Coast Ave.
Lantana, Florida 33464

THE STAR	MONEYSWORTH
World News Corp.	Avant Guarde Media, Inc.
730 Third Avenue	251 West 57th Street
New York, N.Y. 10017	New York, N.Y. 10019

These address and phone accommodation firms also advertise in the following magazines:

MECHANIX ILLUSTRATED
Fawcett Publications, Inc.
1585 Broadway
New York, N.Y. 10036

POPULAR MECHANICS	POPULAR SCIENCE
The Hearst Corp.	Times Mirror Magazines, Inc.
224 West 57th Street	380 Madison Avenue
New York, N.Y. 10019	New York, N.Y. 10017

When you write to any of these publications enclose a check for a dollar and request a sample copy of their magazine and their data on subscription. Usually they will return the check with the sample. If not, it's well worth the dollar you invested.

However, be sure to check the newsstands or your local stationers who carry magazines. You might find the magazines readily available.

One of the suggested layouts for your business cards could be as follows:

XYZ* CORPORATE MANAGEMENT
A Division of UVISCO
(your home address or out of state mail address)
(also put both the out of state and local phone)

Your Name   Marketing/Sales
Title**   Leasing
(President/Vice
President/Executive
Vice President)

(*)   You can use your own initials as part of the corporate title to make it more impressive.
(**) If you use executive vice-president or vice president you can always promote yourself to president later on and gather more publicity.

Please remember that these business cards are designed for a specific purpose—to help give you a professional identity that 'fits' the proposition you will be making to the owner of the building where you want to locate your corporate headquarters.

Later, if you wish, you can add this company to your string of corporations. Meanwhile it's for the limited purpose of obtaining a free suite of offices.

The next step in your operation is to locate target buildings which will suit your purpose. You will also require a particular type of building. Here's how you find them:

Start looking for office buildings which display signs reading: OFFICES FOR RENT followed by a telephone number. This means there is no renting agent on the premises. These are your targets. Move around, find the best looking and latest looking office buildings. Write the addresses of the buildings and the phone number next to it. Take notes about the location—the neighborhood it's in. Look at the building as though you had an appointment with a company in the building. What would be your impression? If it's a good one—put an X next to the address of the building.

Keep doing this till you have a list of about ten buildings.

Your next stop is a large department store. Go to the leather goods section and buy a relatively expensive attache case. Black leather, slim and rich looking. You should spend between $50 and $60 for the case. It's an important tool. Your next stop is in the hardware section where you will pick up some saddle soap.

Go home, saddle soap that attache case and buff it until all the brand-new appearance is gone. It will preserve and protect the leather and yet make it seem well worn but cared for.

When your business cards are ready, you will begin the next phase of your operation. Start calling the numbers of the office buildings on your list.

Remember, your main purpose is to get in touch with the owner of the building—no one else. You may meet resistance. Be prepared for it. Ask for the name of the building owner. You're looking for an individual owner—not a corporation. If there is a rental agent—then forget it and go on to the next number on your list.

If you should meet with some self-important type who refuses to give you the name of the owner, gently explain that you can obtain the necessary information in about ten minutes at the Hall of Records and when you do get in touch with the owner there will be little appreciation of the interference.

Incidentally, when you call—always ask the name of the person to whom you are talking. Ask them to spell it carefully and write it down. You now have a handle on the person. Then ask for the name of the owner. If you get any flack—they know you have their name—and you can gently apply pressure (pleasantly) and you will get your information.

After you have the name—ask if you can speak to this owner. If he or she is not in—ask to speak to the owner's secretary. When you get her—ask for an appointment with the owner. If you're asked what it's about simply say that it has to do with a business proposition concerning the building.

If you have a job, you will have to arrange to meet with your prospects early in the morning, on your lunch hour or late in the afternoon. You could also make a couple of Saturday appointments.

If you have a steady income that is not derived from a job with fixed hours then, of course, you can make the appointments any time you like.

Continue with this activity until you have lined up as many appointments as possible—but be sure to set them up one day apart.

On your appointed day you, and your attache case and business cards, will arrive exactly five minutes early for the appointment. Give your business card to the receptionist and tell her you have an appointment.

The receptionist will either call in your name or take your card in to the owner's office. In either event when you go into his office go directly to him (or her) shake hands—announce your name and (if he or she hasn't been given your card—hand one over).

You will undoubtedly be asked about UVISCO. Just smile and say that it's a venture capital firm but that your company has complete authority then—launch into your story which is as follows:

Your company (Corporate Management) is mainly engaged in leasing and/or selling office buildings and space. You would like consideration of the following proposition:

1. You would establish your company headquarters in his office building.

2. You would undertake to act as his on-the-premises rental agent.

3. You would also undertake to act as building management to oversee all maintenance—tenant problems, etc.

4. At least one member of your staff would be present and available on the premises from 9 to 5:00 each day for current tenant contact and/or conducting prospective tenants on a tour and signing them.

5. Your company would undertake and underwrite the cost of preparation and dissemination of all publicity,

advertising and public relations relative to leasing office space in the building.

In consideration of these activities on his behalf your company would expect the following:

(a) A levy of 2% of all rentals, current or future which would be credited to your account until such time as a year's rental of your company's office space had been satisfied. From that point on, the 2% would be due and payable to your company quarterly.

(b) Since you will, in addition to furnishing your own offices—also furnish several other offices completely— to enhance the rental possibilities, you expect him to provide the telephones and telephone charges, not to exceed $100. per month.

If this meets with his approval you can ask that either a letter of intent or a complete contrat be drawn and you will immediately facilitate the furnishing of the premises.

This is a sound business proposition for the building owner. He will have both a rental agent and building management on his premises—which is an important consideration. It virtually costs him nothing since the 2% levy goes into his own pocket as rent. The most he is out of pocket is the cost of installing the phones and a limit of $100. per month.

Let's suppose, at this point that your prospect asks you for references and the names of other building owners that you have performed this kind of service for. That poses a problem since you obviously can't give him any names.

There are two different ways to handle this kind of a situation:

(1) You can tell him that one of the most important aspects of your type of business is the confidential nature of the relationship you offer clients. That it is, in many respects, the same kind of relationship that doctors and lawyers employ. You can assure him that you would extend him the same courtesy in the event that you established a business relationship with him. However you will be happy to supply him with bank references and—if he wishes—you would have no objection to being bonded during the course of your relationship.

There is nothing to worry about if he does decide to

apply for a bond. The bonding company only investigates to make certain that you do not have a criminal record or a bad credit rating.

Now you will have to determine beforehand whether or not your prospect will accept that kind of an explanation of why you cannot give him the names of former clients. If you do not feel that he will accept this concept then do not attempt to use it. Instead:

(2) Be perfectly honest with him and explain that you haven't had any previous clients. Tell him that what you are doing is really swapping your time and effort on his behalf for office space. That you certainly hope to make money for both of you through sustained effort, publicity and on-the-spot representation. You can also tell him that you will, if he wants, allow yourself to be bonded to protect him against any failing on your part during your relationship.

In many cases you will find that honesty really pays when you're dealing with a prospect. There's nothing underhanded in what you are attempting to do. So if you have a choice—be honest with him. You'll have a much better relationship if you do.

HOW TO SET UP YOUR OWN CORPORATION

Most people are astonished to discover that you can, in most states, set up your own corporation for less than $50.00. It's not difficult. You can obtain the necessary forms from the state capitol, fill them out (they're quite simple), pay the fee and you are incorporated!

Some states require that you advertise your incorporation. There is a corporate kit available which contains your stock certificates, minutes of meetings book and your corporate seal. Any lawyer can tell you where to purchase it. The kit costs about $35.00.

If you would rather have everything done for you, there are, in most cities, special companies that will do everything for you and charge a third of the attorney's fee—about $150.00.

HOW TO OBTAIN A
PRESTIGIOUS PHONE NUMBER

One of the most obvious symbols of success is a business telephone that ends in 00. Generally the distinctive 00 numbers are reserved for large and successful organizations. Every city phone company keeps a certain number of telephone numbers ending in 00 in reserve. They guard them fiercely and you will have to put up a fight to get one.

You start your campaign by requesting the 00 listing through the regular channels. You will be told that there are none left. Ask to be switched to a supervisor. Explain that you are the president of the XYZ Corporation—that you will require at least 3 numbers to begin with and possibly at least four in reserve. You have been told that you cannot have the 00 numbers. The supervisor will tell you that there are none left. You tell the supervisor that you know for a fact that there are reserve 00 numbers that are available. The supervisor will tell you that there are none available.

You then ask to talk to the supervisor's superior. The supervisor will tell you that it won't do any good. You will insist on talking to the superior. Eventually, reluctantly, you will be switched to the superior.

You start all over again by explaining that you are the president of the XYZ Corporation and that you are locating your corporate headquarters in this city. That it will become the hub of your entire organization. Naturally, since you will need at least 3 numbers to begin with and as many as 4 numbers in reserve, you want a number with a 00 ending. Not just for convenience for your clients but also for the prestige which your company deserves.

The supervisor will tell you that it's not possible; that there are no 00 numbers left. You then tell the supervisor that you are quite certain that if U.S. Steel or General Motors were to open headquarters tomorrow that 00 numbers would be found.

If this person will not give you the number then ask to talk to his superior. Just keep pushing up the ladder. They will not be able to refuse to let you talk to their superior because you will always have recourse to letter writing or appearing in person.

Just be confident, polite and continue to push up that ladder and you will, in the end, have your way and your 00 number.

LOOK FOR THE PRESTIGE ADDRESS

Another visible symbol of success is the address of your offices. If possible try to choose buildings that have a name in the address. For example: 19 Grand Army Plaza—27 Forest Way—75 Michigan Boulevard—18 Lincoln Drive—anything other than 25 West 26th Street. If the building has a name that's excellent—for instance, Westinghouse Towers—The Empire State Building—a name that connotes power and that's what you want for your offices if possible. So keep that in mind when you're shopping for a building.

How would you like to have a building named after you or your corporation? It really isn't difficult. Once you develop your capabilities as a rental agent or if your corporation begins to grow to the point where you are a dominant tenant you will probably be able to have the building named The Jones Industry Building or, possibly, just your corporate name.

Your landlord will probably have no objection but he may want something in return. You can then remind him that you and your company are constantly in the news. If the building was named after you or your corporation, every time a news story broke his building would be receiving free publicity.

I have done this, in the past, and you cannot imagine how impressed my prospective clients have been when they arrived at an office building with a brass sign proclaiming it to be the West Corporation Building. The impression is overpowering.

Naturally you can only do this with moderately sized office buildings, but it's well worth the effort in prestige.

GETTING OFFICE FURNITURE FREE

You are now ready for the next phase of the operation. Check the yellow pages for the names and phone numbers of the largest and most aggressive office-furniture-leasing firms. You can usually tell by the size of their display advertising.

Make your calls—remembering that you want to speak to the top executive only. Use the same technique as before. Ask for the name of the person answering the phone.

Set up your appointments one day apart and keep them until you have concluded your deal. Here's the story:

You tell the top executive at the office furniture leasing firm that you will be opening your company's offices at the XYZ Building and that you have a contract to act as renting agent. You tell your contact that you would also like to act as agents for his firm as well since it would be a simple matter, once you have leased a prospective tenant office space, to demonstrate the special benefits that can be obtained from leasing instead of purchasing office furniture.

In addition to eliminating the need for a large cash outlay, there was the additional factor that leasing costs can be deducted as a legitimate business expense.

Your intention is to use your offices and a few other offices as on-the-spot showrooms. The offices could be, in essence, leased 'as is' or—if different furniture was desired—supplied.

The leasing company would then have—a salesman and a showroom—on the premises.

All commission on furniture leasing obtained by your company would be credited against the rental of your company's furnishing for the first six months.

At the end of six months an evaluation would take place. If commissions were less than the six months rental cost your company would pay the balance. If more than the six months' costs the excess would be credited against the next six months.

This is a strong pitch and offers considerable incentive to an office furniture leasing firm because they have nothing to lose and everything to gain.

Let them draw up a contract or a letter of intent and, again, once you have closed the deal, call the other outfits, apologize and ask if you can get back to them at a later date. Keep the list because you will be back.

As soon as your offices (which should be a really large suite of offices) is set and furnished—call in a sign painter and have him paint: (on the front door of the offices)

CORPORATE MANAGEMENT
A Division of UVISCO

Also pick up two plastic (wood grained) office signs for the doors of two offices. One says: VICE PRESIDENT; the other says: PRESIDENT. Screw them into the doors of the two most prominent offices as you pass through the reception area.

You will move into the Vice President's office for now. Later on you will be President and move into the other office.

Be sure to place four listings in the lobby directory:

YOUR NAME	ROOM NUMBER
UVISCO	"
Corporate Management	"
Rental Agents	"
Building Management	"

You are now ready to engage in the next part of your operation. Now that you have a corporate headquarters you can order stationery and supplies. Order simple, thermographed business stationery (on 25% rag bond letterhead and envelopes) using the following format in deluxe Gothic type: (See image building kit for samples.)

CORPORATE MANAGEMENT
A Division of UVISCO

Address   Phone No.

Order 1,000 letterheads and 500 envelopes.
Re-order business cards with your address and phone.

HOW TO GET FREE ACCOUNTING
AND LEGAL SERVICES

Have your secretary check the phone book and then call a local advertising agency and ask them to send an account executive to see you.

When he arrives have your secretary show him into your office, greet him warmly, make him comfortable and ask him to tell you about his advertising agency. He will, at some length. He will also show you samples of the agency's work.

When he's finished with his presentation, ask him about himself—his background—his relationship with the agency. Be attentive—take notes and carefully consider him as a possible recruit for later on.

Then explain to him that your company is making plans to mount an extensive advertising and public relations campaign in the near future. However, at the moment you are only going to initiate a modest recruitment program and a brief P.R. effort. Is his agency willing to take on that kind of limited assignment?

Wanted	Wanted
BRIGHT	**BRIGHT**
YOUNG	**YOUNG**
ATTORNEY	**ACCOUNTANT**
As Corporate	As Corporate
AFFILIATE	AFFILIATE
Free Prestige Office	Free Prestige Office
CALL	**CALL**
00-0000	**00-0000**
Corporate Management	Corporate Management
A Division of	A Division of
UVISCO	**UVISCO**
Address line	Address line

If he says 'yes' then show him these two ads. Have him place these ads in the business connections section of the classified ads or on the financial page of the newspapers you have chosen. You will also ask him to get back to you with agency rates for handling the following publicity releases.

Here's an idea of how the publicity release should be set up. Use your corporate stationery.

PRESS RELEASE*

For Immediate Release   Contact:
Date   (Your new lawyer's
                                    name/your phone)

    (YOUR NAME), vice president of Corporate Management, a subsidiary of UVISCO has announced that as a result of recent corporate expansion, he has retained the services of (LAWYER'S NAME) as corporate counsel. (LAWYER'S NAME) is a graduate of (Name college and Name Law School) (then follow with a brief biography of lawyer).

    Corporate Management has also retained the services of (ACCOUNTANT'S NAME) as corporate financial advisor and tax consultant. (ACCOUNTANT'S NAME) is a graduate of (Name College/University—brief bio, etc.).

    In making the announcement, (YOUR NAME) said,

    "We feel quite fortunate in being able to add these two, personable and qualified professionals to our corporate staff. I am certain they will both make significant contributions to the growth and increased success of Corporate Management."

END

---

*(See Image Building Kit for sample.)

NEWS RELEASE

FOR IMMEDIATE RELEASE   DATE

Corporate Management of (City or Town), a division of UVISCO, has announced the establishment of company headquarters at (XYZ Building/address).

(Your name) vice president of Corporate Management in charge of marketing and sales, said, in a recent interview,

"We are really pleased with our new location and feel particularly honored to have been selected by (name of owner) as building management consultants and authorized rental agents. We are instituting new and innovative approaches to a 'total' leasing concept and towards that end have entered into an agreement with (name of office furniture leasing firm).

We are also in the process of negotiating with several other realty firms with regard to our 'total' leasing concept and expect to conclude new contracts before the end of this month."

END

As accountants and lawyers call in from the ad, it will be time for you to interview bright young attorneys and accountants.

Why are you interviewing them? Because they can be useful to you, in a number of ways. What you are looking for is exactly what you advertised for. A bright young attorney who needs a sound base to operate from. You can offer him a completely furnished office, with secretarial service and his name on the door in gold leaf (as well as in the lobby register) and he can have it rent-free—as a form of a monthly retainer (worth about $250.00 per month) in return for occasional legal services. You will, of course, reimburse him for any out-of-pocket expense. The same deal goes for the young accountant. You want one that's tax-oriented.

When you find the right two, you set them up and then you have another publicity release to send out.

HOW TO GET A LUXURY CAR FREE

Obtain a map of your local area. Using the location of your office as the center, draw a large circle with a radius of approximately 75 miles. Find and mark the location of all of the luxury car dealers within that circle.

When you are finished you will find there are certain clusters of new car agencies. Draw a circle around each cluster. These are 'target' areas. Assign an initial to each 'target' area as -A-B-C-D-E-F etc.

Now select a different car dealer from each target area. For example: A Cadillac dealer in target area "A"—a Lincoln-Continental car dealer in target area "B"—a Mercedes-Benz car dealer in target area "C" and a Jaguar dealer in "D".

You will now call a temporary office help firm and hire a temporary typist-receptionist on a per diem basis.

Have her type individually addressed 'form letters' to all the luxury car dealers as follows:

Car Agency Name   Date
Address
Att: (Name of Owner)

Dear Mr. _____:

    I have reason to believe that I can arrange for the sale of between 27 and 36 new (name of car) for cash, at list price, within the next three months.

    If you can accommodate such an order and would be interested in discussing mutually advantageous terms for such a transaction, please contact my office and let my secretary know when it would be convenient for you to meet me in my office.

    Thanking you for your courtesy in this matter and looking forward to meeting you soon, I remain,

                Very truly yours,
                   (Signature)
                Your name
                Vice President

ABC/nb

Now take the letters that your tempo girl has typed, sign them, seal them up and arrange them in target area groups. Place a small initial in the area where the stamp will go (C for Cadillac, LC for Lincoln-Continental, M for Mercedes and J for Jaguar). When you stamp these letters the initial will disappear. Do not stamp any yet.

Mail these letters on the day that the ads are supposed to appear. That way, the letters will arrive the day after the ads appear in the newspapers. Your ads are more than recruitment ads—they also advertise your company and give the impression that it's a growing concern.

Hire your tempo secretary for the day that the ads will appear. Instruct her to set up the appointments for lawyers and accountants for the following Saturday. Arrange for the appointments to be one hour apart. Also arrange to have her work that Saturday.

Now when your letters reach the car dealers you can also expect calls. Have the calls put through to you immediately. The car dealer will probably come right to the point and ask, "When can we meet?" Tell him, your office in one hour. Each dealer after that should be spaced an hour later than the previous one. Don't make more than 3 appointments for any day. Give the fourth caller an appointment the following day.

When the first car dealer arrives, have your secretary show him into your office. Sit him down and tell him the following:

"Because of my leasing activities in real estate, office furniture and other areas, I will during the next 3 months be in a position to direct the purchase of between 27 and 36 of your top cars, fully loaded, and a full list price. They will be purchased in units of 9 cars at a time. When the deal is consumated— that is, as each 9 car unit is purchased and paid for— I want a check, in my name, for 10% of the total purchase price exclusive of tax."

He will, of course, tell you that it's too much. He will probably offer you 5% (the usual finder's fee).

You counter with 7% and a new car. He'll counter with 4% and a new car. You hold at 7% and a new car. He'll probably come up to 5% and a new car reluctantly. You counter with: 6% and a new car and on all subsequent deals—straight 6% and no car. He'll probably buy it.

You will shake hands and then buzz your secretary and ask her to type up the letter of intent and give her the figures of 6% and a new, fully loaded (make of car) and all subsequent deals straight 6%. You will have furnished her with a form letter previously which reads:

Your name   Date
Address

Dear Mr. (Your Name):

It is my understanding that on this date we have reached the following agreement. That on the day that I receive payment in full for the purchase of nine (9) fully loaded, brand new (year) (make of car) obtained through your efforts, I shall present you with a finders fee which shall include the following: A check made out to your corporation, in the amount that represents 6% of the total purchase (exclusive of tax) and title and license to a brand new, fully loaded (year) (make of car). It is further understand that in all future 9 car unit purchases obtained through your efforts you shall receive a check, made out to your corporation in the amount that represents 6% of the total purchase price and that this shall represent your total finder's fee for that 9 car unit purchase.

_____

Car Dealer's Name
Address

When it's typed up, he signs your copy, you give him his copy with your signature and okay and send him on his way. You go through the same procedure with each dealer you interview. You go to a bottom line of 6% and a new car only as a last resort. Remember you already have one agreement sewn up. Really try for the 10% and then try to hold for the 7% and a new car. Don't worry about winding up with a raft of new cars. If you don't want them you can always sell them.

Now the next phase of your operation, after you have dealt with all the dealers in your first target area is to line up prospects for your special corporation. It's called a Sub S type and is restricted to 10 stockholders. Each one of the stockholders you choose must be in at least a 50% tax bracket because what you are going to offer them is a combination tax shelter, tax break and a brand new fully loaded luxury car for nothing!

I'll explain how it works in a moment but right now you're going to have your secretary send the following letter to a special list of top executives:

The list will be compiled from a Dun & Bradstreet Directory of million plus firms. You will be looking for such firms that are located within a 75-mile radius from your office.

Prospect's Business   Date
Address

Att: Prospect's Name & Title

Dear Mr. _____:

I an writing to you with regard to an unusual legal tax shelter which offers you the unique opportunity to take a large tax deduction legitimately and, at the same time, gives you the pleasure of driving a brand new Cadillac, Lincoln Continental, Mercedes or Jaguar (you name it) for an entire year—and—at the end of the year—owning it outright. Yet it hasn't cost you a penny! Sounds impossible, Mr. _____, doesn't it? Well, it's perfectly true and I'd like an opportunity to demonstrate that truth at your convenience.

Would you send back the enclosed postcard indicating the car you would prefer and giving me a time when we may meet (at my office or yours).

I look forward to hearing from you.

Sincerely,

(Signature)

Your name
Title/

Remember— you have already laid a credibility groundwork with your little publicity campaign. Your name and company may even be familiar to them.

There is an inexpensive way to send out large quantities of individually typed letters. You have to contact one of the many promotion-mailing companies that employ Hooven automatic typewriter equipment. This equipment, in addition to typing in your prospects' name and address in the beginning of the letter will, when programmed, switch to typing a regular form letter, then stop, in the middle and insert your clients' name as:

Most certainly, Mr. Jones, you will agree that this is a significant tax savings for you.

The power of that kind of personalized letter is remarkable. There is no way to determine that it is not typed by your secretary at your office expressly for that particular prospect.

The cost for each letter (in quantities less than 1000) is only 75¢. Now if you are excited by this type of letter writing, and wanted to use them for large mailings, there are companies that have IBM 360 computers that can type 2,000 letters an hour. They are fully equipped with upper and lower case and produce beautifully typed letters. The cost per letter, in large quantities, is about 5¢ a piece! Can you imagine the awesome power you generate by sending out 20,000 personalized letters per day?

Your name, as well as your company name is gaining wider and wider recognition. You should expect, by this time, to have received invitations to receive all the major credit cards.

By now your postcards should be coming in from your prospects. Sort them out so that you have them in units of 9 that are interested in the same kind of car.

Then sit down with your attorney and accountant. Let them clue you in on the ins and outs of the Sub S corporation; as to any limitations in the state where you are located.

In essence what they will tell you is:
1. The corporation can only issue one type of stock.
2. There can only be ten stockholders.
3. They must all live in the same state.
4. Each stockholder must be a person not a corporation.

5. They cannot belong to any other
Sub S corporation.

NOTE: Be sure that your attorney checks the law
on Sub S chapter carefully because there
are modifications passed almost daily.

Now this is what you will explain to your prospects when
you meet them (in addition to the above).

(a) As a stockholder they will be permitted to declare (as
deductions) all depreciation and interest of the
corporation (that is 10%—their 10% of the corp.).
Since there is a 20% depreciation in the first year as well
as a 1/6 (6 year depreciation) and also the allowance
for 1/10th of the interest charges, this represents a
hefty legitimate deduction.

(b) The car will be leased from the corporation (the lease
charges will equal the monthly payments of principal
and interest) and will be a 100% writeoff as a business
expense. Since the stockholder is in the 50% bracket
that means one half of the total sum is deductible.

(c) At the same time the stockholder, under terms of the
leasing agreement owns the car outright at the end of
the year. He can sell the car to a dealer or private party
at the wholesale price for a techinical 'no gain'
transaction and pocket the money which is approximately half the value of the original cost.

The stockholder can start the whole thing all over the next
year—and again, at the end of the year, pocket the money
legitimately. He now has, in his pocket the total cost of that
brand new, luxurious car and it's his—free and clear—to do
what he wants with it.

That's a beautiful deal for anyone in the 50% bracket.

You should have no difficulty selling it and you can look
forward to making a clean 6% each time you set up one of these
special corporations. In addition to your brand new car.

The way it works out (in essence) is this:

The money that each stockholder pays for this share of stock
actually equals one third of the value of his car. Each
stockholder will then lease his car for one year from his own

leasing corporation. His lease charge per month is 1/12th of the balance owed on his car, plus interest.

The stockholder's lease contract gives him the car free and clear at the end of the year.

The leasing corporation uses the money paid in for the stock as the down payment on the cars. With that kind of up-front money there should be no difficulty in arranging for a loan because the cars themselves become collateral.

When you've settled on your first group, have your resident lawyer set up the special Sub S corporation and issue the shares of stock to each member.

Then take your down payment money and open a corporate account at the same bank you opened your personal checking account with. You may be sure, by this time, that the bank manager has heard about you and your company. Now when you open the corporate account for an amount that could be between $30,000. and $40,000. you are a force to be reckoned with and respected as an important depositor.

Now sit down with the bank manager and tell her (or him) that you will be negotiating for the purchase of about $120,000. dollars worth of luxury cars for your leasing corporation. You have more than enough for the down payment and you want to negotiate a loan for the balance, the cars being the collateral, of course. You already have the signed leases from 9 or 10 of your prestigious stockholders—so there is no question that the deal will go through.

The members will, of course, have selected the cars and the appointments they want and you have your orders in your hand when you visit the car dealer. You negotiate for the cars, delivery dates, etc., give the binder and then, if you want, go on to setting up your next deal while you're waiting for the first corporate cars to be delivered. You could, if you wished, keep on making these deals over and over and probably make $50,000. or more the very first year, without trying too hard. Or, you could set your deals so that in addition to cash you wound up with a free Cadillac, Lincoln-Continental, Mercedes and a Jaguar.

When you receive your first check from the car dealer, when the deal has been consumated, pay back your loans at both banks, relax and enjoy your new role in your brand new car.

HOW TO LIVE IN A LUXURIOUS
APARTMENT AT LESS THAN
THE RENTAL OF AN ORDINARY ONE

You will generally find, in or near most cities, several, so-called 'luxury apartment complexes' which offer a wide range of extra conveniences. Many of them have swimming pools, health clubs and even 9 hole golf courses. There are uniformed doormen, security guards, secretarial services and, all in all, most of the amenities that are the usual privilege of the rich.

While it is true that some of the apartments are pegged at a really high rental, many of them are not as high as you would expect. Many people are astonished to discover that the rental on some two-bedroom luxury apartments are not significantly higher than the rental of an ordinary two-bedroom garden apartment.

For example: a garden apartment in the suburbs of New York will rent for about $350.00 per month. There are two-bedroom apartments in luxury apartment complexes for just $500.00 per month. That's only $150.00 per month difference and yet the added facilities and the prestige such living offers is well worth the difference.

However, many landlords find it difficult to rent these apartments and, as an inducement they sometimes offer a bonus of two or three months free rental for a tenant who will sign a two year lease. That savings, amortized over a period of 24 months would bring the cost down to less than $450.00 per month. That means it would cost $100.00 per month more for that rich living.

There is, however, a way to reduce that rental even more. If we assume that you have already acquired the skills necessary to pursue your 'second' career—you have something to offer the landlord.

If he has empty apartments, which is a strong possibility, he's missing the rental on them anyway and has little to lose and much to gain if you offer him part of your rental in services rather than cash. If you're into interior decoration, or you're a tax specialist or even an investment counselor, he could certainly use your services. If he's impressed with you (and he should be if you've done your homework) then there is a good chance that he will accept your offer and take half the rental in services rendered over a 24 month lease.

You then wind up with your luxury apartment at about $225.00 per month which is less than the cost of an ordinary garden apartment. You not only have a really prestigious address, you have all the luxurious benefits as well. Swimming pool, tennis courts, golf course—all the security you could want for your family—everything.

And you thought you couldn't live like a millionaire on an ordinary income.

BARTERING YOUR SERVICES FOR EVERYTHING YOU NEED IS GOOD BUSINESS FOR EVERYONE

When you offer to barter your particular skills and services you're simply engaging in the kind of business that this entire nation started with. There's nothing wrong with the concept. It's good business for both of you. The man you deal with is merely exchanging his goods for your services.

When I first started out in business for myself I had no difficulty in getting just about every symbol of success through barter. That's how I got my first, really decent wardrobe, my first well-appointed, luxury car, my first suite of offices and eventually a building with my name on the front of it.

AN ALTERNATIVE PLAN FOR
OBTAINING OFFICE SPACE
FOR LITTLE OR NO RENT

I had a good friend who was just not comfortable with the idea of becoming a rental agent for a landlord in return for free office space. So I gave him another plan which might also interest you.

In just about every city there are office rental companies who offer special rental services to small business firms. These office rental companies will take over entire buildings or floors and turn each floor into suites of offices with a central reception area. Anyone can rent a single office or several connected offices on each floor. The offices are fully furnished and have telephones that are connected to the central switchboard manned by an attractive, intelligent woman who acts as your receptionist and telephone secretary. The cost for everything (except your outgoing phone calls) is about $200.00 per month.

You couldn't hire a receptionist for that kind of money, let alone a furnished office that gives you an address and a phone number instantly.

Now there is a way to reduce that rental even more. Certainly the people who run that rental service company are in need of services. You could barter your services as a tax consultant, interior decorator, investment counselor and so on, for at least half the rent. That would mean that you were now paying $100.00 per month for your fancy office complete with receptionist and telephone operator.

You can't garage your car in New York City for that kind of money per month.

HOW TO CREATE POWERFUL
PERSONAL SELLING TOOLS

Quite a number of interesting ideas are presented by Robert Ringer in his unique book "WINNING THROUGH INTIMIDATION" and I recommend that you read it.

One of the ideas he presents is something that he did when he first started out as a real estate broker and had limited credentials and limited accomplishments. Did this deter Mr. Ringer? Not in the least. He simply had a stunning, full color brochure created which talked about him in glowing terms. The cover of this unique brochure carred a full color map of the world with certain areas pinpointed as the location of major real estate transactions. While the exact nature of these real estate deals is not disclosed (nor is the person who consumated these deals disclosed) the implication is that Robert Ringer is the hero. After all, the entire brochure, with the exception of the text on the services of a real estate broker's methods and techniques, is about Robert Ringer.

Ringer states that the cost of the brochure, though expensive (about $5.00 each), was well worth it because it was, in many cases, the key factor in million dollar real estate deals.

Ringer felt that there was nothing more impressive to a client, some 2,000 miles away, who had never heard about Robert Ringer, to receive a full color brochure that was comparable to an annual report from U.S. Steel.

There is little doubt that Ringer is a master of the art of 'winning through intimidation' (a technique that you should also master to live like a millionaire on an ordinary income).

A variant of this idea of a personal, full color brochure, which I have employed on behalf of clients with considerable success, is a color slide presentation on you and your company. This can be transformed into a film strip with professional narration added on a sound track. It's not really difficult to do and can be a lot of fun to assemble. Some of the color slides will be stock slides of your city skyline, points of interest, bridges and impressive buildings, which can be purchased at most major camera stores. The other color slides will be those of you and your associates in your suite of offices, in outdoor shots, where you're arriving in your chauffeured limousine for an important appointment at some impressive building which ostensibly houses your clients, and there could be a montage of news stories about your firm and its activities. In all, it could be an impressive, colorful documentary about you and your company richly described by a professional narrator in a tone of voice reserved for a major affiliate of I.B.M. or DuPont.

You can obtain the services of a professional narrator through your local radio or TV station. If you give the salient information about yourself and your company to one of the copywriters at the radio station, you will receive an excellent narrative for your narrator.

The cost, for the service of both these professionals is really nominal (approximately $100 each). Again, you could always barter your services if you wished and possibly obtain their services in return for yours.

If you like the idea, and really want to do it in a big way, you could contact AFTRA (American Federated Television and Radio Actors) or SAG (Screen Actors Guild) and get a well known personality to do your narration. This would elevate your prestige sky high.

In any event, if you wish to do it yourself, then you can either purchase (possibly with barter) or lease the equipment which will synchronize sound and color slide presentation. The lease cost would be about $20.00 per month. When you were finished with your work you dim the lights, push the button, and sit back and watch yourself and your company in living color and sound.

The first shot (with majestic music underneath) is a long, panoramic view of the city skyline with a vivid blue sky and fleecy white clouds and then, the superimposed title appears:

YOUR NAME
and
UVISCO INDUSTRIES
Presents

(Next frame—long aerial shot of the city at dawn)
THE
SEARCH
FOR EXCELLENCE

Now, with a four beat, brief passage from the soundtrack of 2001 that comes up and then fades underneath the narrator, the nice, round voice (reminiscent of early Orson Wells) begins to tell the dramatic story of your early beginnings and your rise to power and position.

If the presentation was keyed carefully it could also be used as a recruitment device for bringing bright new people into your organization.

It could also be modified slightly for an investor presentation and could be the hinge-pin in an overall expansion plan which requires considerable capital.

However you used it, you can be certain that it would be a powerful personal selling tool that could be used over and over again with tremendous effectiveness.

HOW TO CREATE A POWERFUL FINANCIAL STATEMENT LEGALLY

I will stress the word legally here because there are strict rules and severe penalties in every state with regard to the submission of fraudulent financial statements (or personal balance sheets).

So be absolutely certain that everything you state in your financial statement is true and accurate, to the best of your knowledge.

Now before you become discouraged at the bad news, here's the good news. There is a perfectly legal way to show considerable assets legally and aboveboard.

The key to the technique I am about to describe is the use of accurate footnotes which clearly put the reader of this financial statement on notice as to exactly what you are stating.

Let's suppose, at this moment, that you have moved ahead with your original corporation; that you have added the leasing corporation, and that you have established a certain eminence via public relations and publicity.

You feel that you are ready to move into the higher air where the big money people are playing their money game. To do that, you will need an excellent financial statement that puts you in the running with high assets.

Now even though you might have one or two luxury cars, several bank accounts as well as other assets, they don't seem to add up to the kind of money we're talking about.

There is, however, something else. You are the founder and major stockholder in your original corporation. Let's say that you have 500,000 shares in this corporation. (You can pay a mil (1/10 of a cent) per share and that doesn't matter.) You have every right to assign a fair market value to those shares. Fair market value is the price that an outside observer would think that he might have to pay if he purchased the assets of the corporation today.

It doesn't matter what you paid to set up this corporation. In the eyes of the world you are a successful corporation—and in many respects you are. In light of that, who is to say that your shares are not worth 50¢ each? That certainly is a modestly conservative figure and would be acceptable by most people.

So now, your personal balance sheet shows that you own 500,000 shares of stock in your corporation which translates into $250,000.00 plus the shares you hold in your leasing corporations at 50¢ each.

The footnotes must clearly state that these various investments are valued on a fair market value basis and do not necessarily bear a relationship to the original cost of your investment. The fact is that this type of financial statement will be acceptable to 85% of the people it is presented to.

The irony of the whole thing is the fact that if you have been following the plan and are becoming successful your shares in your corporation are worth more than 50¢!

HOW TO IMPRESS A CLIENT
AND MAKE A BIG DEAL STICK

There are really no certainties in this world. Just because a client signs a paper, a contract or an agreement, does not mean that he will always honor his word. Everyone in the business world has suffered the traumatic experience of a perfectly valid agreement falling apart because a client suddenly changes his mind. Of course there is always the recourse of suit for breach of contract, but this is really not a solution. No one really wins a lawsuit, and the repercussions of a suit do little for your reputation within the business community.

An excellent technique that I have used to cement many of the major financial dealings I have been responsible for is this:

Immediately after the completion of the deal I send the client a beautiful green plant with a card that says,

"As this plant greens and grows, so will our relationship. Kindest regards."

Not one of the clients I have sent that plant and card to, has ever cancelled a deal.

HOW TO SET UP YOUR OWN ASSOCIATION OR COMMITTEE

Most people have no idea that it's both permissible and legal to set up your own association or committee. You may assign it virtually any high sounding name you wish—so long as it doesn't conflict with an established association or committee.

If it's set up to deal with a problem that concerns you, there is every reason to suppose that you could really accomplish a lot with it.

However, our concern, at the moment, is prestige. Let's suppose, for the sake of argument, you decided to set up the AMERICAN ASSOCIATION OF CONCERNED PARENTS. You could have letterheads made up, with your name as President of the Association and send out publicity releases, invite membership, hold meetings and presto! you are widely recognized in your new role.

The fact that you are self appointed or that you created the association, never seems to come up. Didn't you ever wonder where all those associations and committees came from? Now you know.

THE SUBLIMINAL VISIBLE
SYMBOLS OF SUCCESS

Subliminal means just below the level of consciousness. The visible symbols of success we are going to talk about are seen by other people but the impact takes place without any conscious realization. It's similar to the behaviorism that was exhibited by Pavlov's dog. Whenever it was fed, a bell would ring. Later, all the doctor had to do was ring the bell and the dog salivated without any food being present.

Our advertising media, television and radio has conditioned most people the way Pavlov's dog was conditioned. Most people tend to associate success with certain subtle symbols. For example, at a meeting, one of the executives takes out a $20.00 Cross pen to make notes. That fact registers. Not consciously, but it adds a 'plus' note to the estimate of that particular executive.

A blue sapphire ring on a well manicured hand will register a 'plus' note. Purchased wholesale or brought back from the Orient, that kind of a ring could cost as little as $175.00 but it can make an impact worth thousands.

I have a friend who wears oversized, solid gold cuff links that impart an aura to his handmade french cuff shirts (with monogram, of course).

Solid gold cigarette lighters, British cigarettes, handmade shoes, superbly tailored clothes—all the symbols of success do something to us as well as to people we meet. They also make us feel successful, as well. And when we feel successful we also act successful and that is part and parcel of living like a millionaire on an ordinary income. If you feel and act the part you will be the part you're playing.

HOW TO BUY A LUXURIOUS HOME
WITHOUT ANY DOWN PAYMENT

Now that you have the clothes, the luxury car, the well known company and the rapidly growing reputation, it's time for you to think about living in a really luxurious home— something in the $100,000.00 to $150,000.00 class.

Pick one of the posh, outlying areas, some distance from your corporate headquarters. Look up real estate agencies in that area. Call a few and ask if they have anything available in the $100,000. to $200,000. class. You may be certain there are several. Particularly when you say that you're looking for an older house rather than a modern one. You see the older house is more likely to be overpriced. It's also owned by someone, generally who wants to get rid of it at a fancy price.

Remember that prices in real estate have become inflated during the past ten years. If the asking price is $100,000.00 it's safe to assume that the asking price ten years ago was around $50,000.00 to $60,000.00

Older houses, in that price class, were really well built, so it's quite reasonable to ask about an older house. The real estate agency will most certainly have one or two of the 'impossibles' and will be delighted at the thought of moving one of them, at long last. He will describe one or two that seem to be what you're looking for and you will thank him and say you'll call him for an appointment, as soon as you're free.

Now you can sit down with your resident attorney and let him earn a little of his retainer. Naturally you'll reimburse him for out-of-pocket expenses. You tell him about the real estate agency and the houses he described. If he has some free time, and it's a nice day, ask him to visit the real estate agency.

His story is that he was passing through the area and liked the look of it. He'd been thinking about buying a home for his family and wondered if the real estate agent had an 'interesting' buy. When the agent asked him the price range he was interested in, he would say 'something in the neighborhood of $100,000.00—but only if it was a real 'buy'.

After selecting a few index cards from his file, the real estate agent would take your attorney for a tour of 'possible' homes. During the tour your bright young attorney would note the location of the various homes he was shown, make notes about the prices that were asked and, when the journey was over, would tell the agent that he would be in touch.

After leaving the agent, your attorney would then visit the town or village hall and after a brief discussion with the village clerk or the property clerk would then examine the property maps, the recorded deeds and learn everything about the property he was interested in. Everything means everything from the time it was purchased from the Indians or staked out in the original land rush.

He'll be able to find out exactly how much the present owner paid for the property, how much taxes he pays and whether there are any encumbrances, judgments or mortgages on it.

When your attorney returns to your office with all the data you are now ready to put your plan into full gear. You drive out, in your luxury car looking exactly like a wealthy, top executive of a highly successful corporation.

When you arrive in the area you call the owner of the home you have selected, ask for an appointment to see the place and, in all events, arrange to see him that day. He will undoubtedly see you, particularly if his home has been on the market for some time. Taxes and mortgage payments can make any man anxious to get rid of a home he no longer wants, particularly if he thinks he can make a real killing.

You explain to him that your company has transferred you to this area and you want a home that's appropriate to your station in life; one that will be ideal for entertaining and this seems to be it. However, you'll know better after you have been through it.

After the tour you tell him that you would like to make the transaction as quickly as possible and, since you will be paying cash, you want the lowest possible price he can give you. Remember you know the actual value of the house and exactly what he paid for it. You can drive a really hard bargain and really bring down the price. He's thinking of the cash and the fact that he has to keep paying money out as it stands empty.

You will get the rock bottom price.

You then shake hands on the deal and tell him that you will be back to confirm everything as soon as you have a firm committment from your company as to the permanent nature of your residency in this area. You're quite sure that you will be, but you just want to make it an absolute certainty before you invest that sum of money.

You allow a day to pass before contacting him again, then call and arrange to see him. When you meet you tell him that your company will not make a committment as to the permanence of your residency until you have achieved the necessary volume of sales in this area. Naturally he will be disappointed. You assure him that you really want the house and that you have an alternative plan. You suggest a lease with an option to buy, at the agreed upon price, within one year.

Now since you have already established the price—let's say that it's $100,000.00—the rule of thumb is 1% a month—or $1,000.00 per month. However, you happen to know that his mortgage and taxes equal $700.00 a month. That's the rental you bargain for. You also try to get an agreement that the rental will apply towards the purchase price. He may balk at that and only allow half.

Accept it. You're getting a bargain, particularly since you have brought the original price down from $150,000.00 to $100,000.00.

Now you can move in, and enjoy your luxurious home and—if you really like it—and things go well with you in your corporate activities, you should have little trouble in arranging for a mortgage for the property.

However, if you can't and the owner doesn't want to continue the arrangement, you've lived for a whole year, like a millionaire at a modest rental. And you can move into your next mansion by repeating the same procedure.

Sometimes you can make a deal like this which, for one reason or another, includes furnishings. In most cases the home will be empty.

HOW TO FURNISH YOUR NEW MANSION

Here's how to completely furnish your home at modest cost and with free advice and counsel from a professional interior decorator.

Use your contact with your office-furniture leasing company. They will put you in touch with a company that leases all of the furnishings for posh apartments and homes. He will also give you added credibility by mentioning that you are a business associate.

Most of these home-furniture leasing firms have an interior decorator on the staff who will at no charge, assist you in creating the proper environment in excellent taste.

You will wind up with a beautifully furnished home for a modest monthly fee which will, of course, be billed to your corporation.

Now the interesting part is this: if you can show that the mansion is actually a corporate entity, that is primarily used for entertaining clients of the corporation, there is every reason to believe that you can write off some of the cost of the furniture lease as well as the overall maintenance of the mansion.

THE CHAUFFEURED LIMOUSINE

One of the really impressive symbols of success is the chauffeured limousine. If you ever want to make an impression on a client, a prospect or a political leader, arrange to have them picked up by a smartly uniformed chauffeur in a luxurious new limousine and brought to your home or office. The cost is surprisingly modest—just about twice the cost of having a cab pick them up—but the impression is worth a million dollars.

Limousine services are available almost everywhere. You'll find them listed in the yellow pages of your telephone directory. Some firms offer Rolls Royce limousines with chauffeur which comes a little higher.

One of the first things that I did, when my corporate ventures began to make considerable demands on my time, was to acquire a superb new Lincoln Town car. I hired a personable young man as my personal assistant and chauffeur.

This limousine and chauffeur not only impresses my clients, it also gives me extra time. I am now free to work in the back of the car without disturbance, as I am driven to one or more of the meetings I attend each day.

This also permits me to arrive refreshed and well prepared for each meeting instead of tired and irritable due to the pressures of traffic and the endless searching for a parking lot with available space.

HOW TO GET VIP TREATMENT

V.I.P. treatment is another important symbol of success that is not only thoroughly enjoyable but also impresses clients and business associates.

I have enjoyed V.I.P. treatment for years through a very simple maneuver. I always had my secretary call, well in advance to inform the maitre d' and the headwaiter that the chairman of the board of the British-American Publishing Corporation, would be arriving with a party of six or seven on such and such a day. She would arrange for a special table, name my favorite wines, etc. Then the day before I was to arrive she would call again, and confirm all the arrangements with the maitre d' and the headwaiter. They were really prepared when I arrived with my party. One of my executive staff would move up quickly before we reached the maitre d' and inform him that Mr. Steven West had arrived with his party. He would point me out to the maitre d' and then tip him liberally to take special pains with me and my guests.

When we arrived, the plush rope was downed quickly and we were escorted to our table with a lot of deference. This sort of thing took place at all the top restaurants and before long my name was in the special book each of these restaurants keeps for V.I.P.'s from the arts, cinema, social register and the business world.

That same kind of V.I.P. treatment was given me by all the major airlines here and abroad simply by having my secretary call in advance and inform them that the Chairman of the Board of British-American Publishing Corporation would be traveling with them on such and such a flight. She would give them my required menu for my meals, my favorite wines, liqueurs and desserts. The result was that I not only flew first class—but with my personal tastes catered—at no extra charge!

In addition to that kind of V.I.P. treatment which you can enjoy just as I do, there is the availability of special clubs that you can join for about $100.00 per year. United Airlines has the 100 Thousand Mile Club and American Airlines offers the Ambassador Club.

As a member you have access, at any time, to plush conference rooms, offices, telephones and superb facilities for freshening up at airports throughout the nation. The only qualifications necessary are that you are an executive who flies their airlines from time to time throughout the year. It certainly beats sitting out in a noisy, crowded airport waiting for your plane to come in.

When I first joined the 100,000 Mile Club they sent me a placque for my wall (another visible symbol of success) which joined the others on the wall of my office.

WRITING AS A STATUS SYMBOL

Writing virtually anything can provide you with more symbols of success. When I was establishing myself as a Merger and Acquisitions Specialist, I wrote and published a newsletter called WEST ON WALL STREET which was a considerable help in establishing my expertise in the field. It gave me access to the top executives in many major corporations and was one of the keys to the successful corporate structure I eventually erected.

Writing and publishing a book is another way to create a powerful symbol of success. You can have a hard-cover, 200-page book printed and bound (in limited quantities) for less than $5,000.00. Can you imagine the power of sending a prospective client an autographed copy of your book? Not only is he flattered by the attention but your credentials as an expert are established firmly in his mind. The book also becomes part of your news release material.

As an established author and an authority on a particular subject you can produce weekly columns or articles for newspapers or magazines—a highly visible symbol of success.

THE PRIVATE PLANE

One of the things I discovered when I was starting out to make my first million was the power of arriving for an appointment in a privately chartered aircraft.

I had an important meeting with a group of investors in Pennsylvania and they were going to meet me at the airport. Instead of taking a scheduled airline I arranged for a pilot and aircraft to take me there.

When we landed, the pilot really gave me the V.I.P. treatment, salute and all. My group of investors were really impressed and the meeting was a complete success.

After the meeting and luncheon, they took me back to the airport, where my pilot and plane were waiting and I took off in a blaze of glory.

Would you believe that the entire round trip flight, including stand down time only cost me $150.00? That flight paid me back a thousandfold not only in terms of prestige but in terms of the success of that meeting. The going cost is approximately 65¢ per mile plus waiting time.

HOW TO GET POLITICAL POWER

All right. You're settled into your new home, with the luxurious car in the driveway; your corporation is running smoothly—why not move into another field that will, in addition to employing your mansion effectively, also provide you with fun and—more importantly—power.

I'm speaking of politics, of course. This is an ideal field for someone like you. I don't mean, at this stage, that you should run for office. That's premature. I mean that you should become involved in politics; develop some fundamental understanding of how the political parties function. Read the papers, listen to people, find out who the "key" people are. Not the elected officials but the party chairmen, the district leaders and so forth.

Your task at this point is to gather information. Test the political wind. Is the party in power likely to stay in power or is there a possibility that events at the state or federal level may weaken the party in power? Try to project the future. Are things happening now that will have a powerful effect at the next election. What kind of an election is it? Whose jobs are up for re-election? Who are the candidates?

The most important (to you) is the question of political issues because you can become involved with an issue in a way that will make you an uncommitted political power. That simply means that you will have (if you are successful) the power to deliver a certain number of votes to a particular candidate when the time is right. Here's how you do it:

Let's say there is a certain issue that affects a lot of people; it's caused a lot of talk but no one has really done anything concrete about it.

Investigate that issue. Find out everything you can about it. Listen to all sorts of people and their opinions. When you have gathered enough information, sit down with your resident lawyer and discuss the legal aspects of the issue. If taxes are involved, sit down with your resident tax man and get some expert input.

You should have, by this time, made a list of people who are deeply concerned with this issue and who will, with the right leadership, work to do something about it. Your next step is:

1. Invite these key people to your home for a special 'get-together' to discuss the issue.
2. Form a special committee of these people.
3. Give each of them printed copies of a special petition you will have had drawn up.
4. Ask each of them to form a 'petition' committee which they will head up. Each committee will be entrusted with the task of obtaining signatures on the petitions. Your goal is a really immense petition.

After the meeting you will send out publicity releases about the formation of the committee and your strong determination with the help of (name your basic members) your committee to develop one of the largest petitions in history. You are now on your way.

If there is an election in the wings you will invite the political leader of the strongest party to visit you at your home. You will question him as to his candidates attitude towards your issue.

The leader knows who you are and whom you are representing. He is fully aware that you have a certain political 'clout' and if he feels it's strong enough he will assure you that his candidate will mention the issue in his campaign.

You will tell the political leader that's not good enough. His candidate will have to make the issue a plank in the political platform. Which means that you want the party to back it as well as the candidate.

This is strong stuff—but if you carry it off you have real dynamite to carry back to your next committee meeting. When you tell them the concession you have wangled from the party (and when the candidate does make his next announcement) you are then in a position to issue your committee's public endorsement of the candidate.

That means you will 'deliver' the votes for that candidate and that is the name of the game in politics. Your ability to deliver votes will mark you as a power to reckon with.

Regardless of whether the candidate wins or loses you have accomplished a great deal. You have solidified your position as the leader of the people in your fight for the issue, and you will continue to fight on.

If the candidate is elected you have become a hero in both camps and will, undoubtedly, be offered a modestly lucrative post which requires little of your time but a regular income. This is part of the 'patronage' system which is enjoyed by the political party in power.

On or about this time—since you are a well known public figure—you will be offered the post of local chairman of one of the major, national health agencies such as Red Cross, March of Dimes, Muscular Dystrophy, etc. You will accept the post and, instead of being just a figurehead, you will be a full-time powerhouse of energy. You will speak, quite frequently; form effective committees and really move your campaign into high gear.

The continuous resulting publicity will be excellent for you. There is nothing more effective than public service work and publicity.

Your committee is not disbanded. It meets quite regularly (with you at the head) in your luxurious home. You sift through the issues and sure enough—there's a hot potato that you can get your committee fired up about—and off you go again.

You keep this up and long about the half way mark to the next election you are going to be given serious consideration as a candidate because you're well known, well liked, you speak well—you move people—and you can win votes. More importantly—once in office you will not fade into the woodwork—you'll be a mover and a shaker and that means you will go up the political ladder.

Now when the time comes that you are offered a candidacy—think it over carefully. If you will be up against a popular, well entrenched incumbent—forget it. You cannot afford a defeat at the beginning of your political career. Decline gracefully and offer to help whatever candidate they choose. However—if your opponent is new—as you are—and on the same level—take the candidacy because you can win it.

One good strong win is all you need to start you on a political career that can have an astonishing future. If that's what you want—reach out and take it—because it can be a wonderful life.

THE FREE VACATION

Expensive vacations are another facet of living like a millionaire (as well as a symbol of success) and there is a simple way to have the kind of vacation you have always dreamed about without paying for it. Remember that committee you formed? Well, it can be valuable in more ways than just political power. You sit down with the head of a good sized travel agency and explain that as the chairman of the XYZ Committee for The Issue, you want to reward your committee people with a special group-plan vacation package. Naturally you will discuss the size of the 'finders fee' with him or her. That can be as much as half the agency commission which is usually 7½% for travel and 10% for hotel accommodations. That can come to a tidy sum, depending on the size of your group. You might start with a Hawaiian vacation because there are no passports involved and it is exotic and far away.

You get all the details and then you prepare a special newsletter and inform all of your committee people about the special vacation and get them to sign up. Do it far enough in advance so that people can plan on it and make arrangements to leave. Naturally you and your mate ride free.

AUTOMOBILE PRESTIGE SYMBOLS

A distinctive license plate (one with your initials) is another symbol of success. It's not difficult to obtain. Just apply to the State Bureau of Motor Vehicles. You have to pay a slight additional fee—usually $10 and generally, you have to have a clean driver's license (no offenses within 16 months). Often the special license if there are no offenses meanwhile—is yours year in and year out. You merely keep renewing it.

It's surprising that even though most people know this is how it's done, they are still impressed with the special license plate. They can't help it, somehow. Particularly when the plate is attached to an expensive car.

People are also impressed when they find that you have a telephone in your car. It's not that expensive. About $50.00 a month and the charges for calling are only slightly higher than your regular calls. I've always had phones in my cars as a matter of practicality. It not only makes me readily available to my people when I'm on the road but it also permits me to conduct business while I'm driving.

CHAPTER FOUR

THE
ART OF
EMPLOYING
CREDIT

This is one of the most important chapters in this book. Why? Because it deals with a concept of credit that can easily change your life for the better.

It changed my life. You see, when I started out to discover what made the rich of this world different from any other class of people I came across a new concept that really startled me.

I had always thought of credit the way most people do: that if you had 'credit' you could borrow money to pay bills and then worry about how you were going to pay back the money you borrowed. It just seemed to be a way of turning a lot of little money problems into one big money problem. Or, in the case of borrowing money to buy a major appliance, install a new oil burner, buy a new car, or a new home—you just extend your money worries over a longer period of time.

The rich, I discovered, don't think that way at all. They borrow money to make money. They use credit to make a profit. That's the way to get rich and that's the way to get richer. That's absolutely true. I know because that's one of the ways I became a millionaire.

Now, if this sounds a little strange to you, hang in there, you'll understand exactly what I mean in a moment.

HOW TO EARN 17% INTEREST

As I was moving slowly up the ladder towards my goal, I found myself with $30,000.00 that was free and clear so I thought about investing in something that would give me a real return on my money. Now I realized that I could put it into a 'certificate of deposit' account with the bank and draw an effective 6% per year which would mean that I'd make $1,800.00 on my money which isn't bad. It's safe—I can't lose it—the money is insured. But that wasn't what I wanted. I wanted a really good return on my money.

So I thought about the stock market, but frankly that seemed risky. I didn't know too much about it at the time and I decided against it. But brokerage houses really fascinated me so I went to a really good firm on Wall Street, sat down with an intelligent 'customer's man' and told him what I had in mind.

He said, "Bonds." Then he showed me that relatively safe utility company bonds payed 10% and I was really impressed. I could make $3,000.00 on my $30,000.00 with very little risk. But he laughed and said, "Why make $3,000.00 when you can make $5,100.00 with the same investment?"

"How? Just tell me how!" I said quickly and he explained that I could buy $100,000.00 worth of bonds by using my $30,000.00 as a down payment and the brokerage house would lend me $70,000.00 at 7%.

It worked out this way: The bonds paid back $10,000.00 in interest. I paid the broker $4,900.00 in interest charges and that left me with a net profit on the deal of $5,100,00 (less broker fees) which, when I added it up, meant that my original $30,000.00 had earned an actual interest of 17%.

In other words I had made money by borrowing money with little or no risk. In addition I made even more money because I sold the bonds for more than I had paid for them.

USING OTHER PEOPLE'S MONEY

This is an important concept which, if you become fully familiar with, can make a considerable amount of money for you. It's the concept that you always use OPM (other people's money) for investment.

There are many different ways to legally make money with OPM. For example, did you know that you may legally have up to 35 investors in a private corporation and not be obligated to file with the SEC (Security Exchange Commission)? While this exemption holds true in most states it's a sound idea to check with your attorney before setting up this corporation.

GETTING CONTROL OF A PUBLIC COMPANY

Here's how you could use such a corporation to your advantage (as well as your investors). Let's suppose you meet the chief executive of a large, publicly held corporation who is also the controlling stockholder. This executive tells you that he's tired and would like to retire. However, the market is in a depressed state and since there is a limit to the amount of stock that he can sell at any given time he simply has to wait.

Now you sound him out and come to an agreement wherein you will find a corporation which will be glad to purchase his controlling shares for an agreed-upon sum of $250,000.00.

Since you are well known in your financial circles as a successful, rising young executive with many ties to the financial world, it would be fairly simple to round up a group of investors who would invest from $5,000.00 to $10,000.00 in this new corporation you will found.

For a nominal sum of money you can take a 25% to 50% ownership of this new corporation which, with the $250,000.00 capital, you would take control of the multi-million dollar corporation. You would, with that simple operation, be the controlling shareholder of this corporation, which controls the public corporation.

This operation is known as Private Placement in which one uses a Private Placement Memorandum. If you're interested in this kind of an operation check it out with your lawyer.

SELLING YOUR OWN STOCK

There is another way to raise a considerable sum of money from a lot of small investors. That's through use of the Regulation "A" Public Offering rule. This Regulation "A" permits you to sell up to $500,000.00 of securities to an unlimited number of investors. You can do this by filing a simple prospectus with the regional office of the Securities Exchange Commission. Your financial statement does not have to be certified. It's safe to assume, with the absence of public offerings these days, that you will probably have your 'go-ahead' in 30 to 60 days and you can act as your own underwriter and sell to a wide range of investors.

A SYSTEM THAT MAKES MONEY
FOR EVERYONE

Here's another hypothetical case. Suppose I had ten friends with money to invest and they asked me to find them an investment that paid at least 12% a year. Let's suppose that each of them had $20,000.00 to invest and I guaranteed them a return of $200.00 per month starting with the first month (30 days) after their original investment.

They would receive the $200.00 per month for 12 consecutive months and then get back their original $20,000.00. They put up the money, I went to my friend at the brokerage house, gave him the $200,000.00, borrowed $600,000.00 at 7% and purchased $800,000.00 worth of bonds.

Then I went to my bank, arranged for a passbook loan for $24,000.00, took it to another bank and opened a special savings account. I gave the bank instructions to withdraw $2,000.00 per month from the account and send each investor $200.00 on the first of each month for 12 consecutive months.

When the year was up I sold the bonds and the final result was this:

Brokerage House:	$600,000.00	(loan repayment)
	42,000.00	(interest)
		642,000.00
Investors	200,000.00	
		200,000.00
		842,000.00
Bonds Yield		
Principal and interest		880,000.00
Gross Profit		38,000.00
Less Interest to Investors		24,000.00
Net Profit to me		$14,000.00

I made $14,000.00 on an investment of $24,000.00 which I borrowed from the bank! That's a return of about 60% on the money. The ten investors made more than 12% because they had their interest payments each month. If they deposited in their savings account each month they would have piled up additional interest by the end of the year.

I now had ten happy investors who were ready to buy my next offering which was a highly interesting transaction. This time I asked that each of them put up $30,000.00 and that for that investment I would pay each of them 12% per year, the same deal as before. This time, of course, they would receive $300.00 per month on the first of each month for 12 consecutive months.

When I went back to the brokerage firm I bought $300,000.00 worth of bonds and resisted his offer to raise it to a million because I had other plans.

I took the paid-in-full bonds to my bank and used them as collateral to borrow $240,000.00 I opened a special savings account and deposited $57,000.00 in it ($40,000.00 of the $240,000.00 and $17,000.00 from a passbook loan from my personal savings account).

I instructed the bank to pay each of the investors $300.00 per month and to pay the bank to pay itself (the $1,600.00 a month interest on the $240,000.00 I had borrowed.)

I now had a year's breathing room with my investors and the bank taken care of and $200,000.00 to make my first big venture in acquiring control of a publicly held (OTC—Over The Counter) corporation.

Here's how I used the plan in an interesting way.

I had met this man who had originally founded the corporation—manufacturing electromechanical clutch and brake components—and built it into a sound little company which eventually 'went public' during the stock market boom days in the middle of the '60's. The stock had traded as high as $20.00 per share during the boom but then sank down into relative obscurity. It wasn't even listed in the daily trading sheets. Stockbrokers, if you asked, gave quotes of about 75¢ to $1.00 per share.

The controlling stockholder, the man I was talking to, was also chairman of the board of directors and was paid a salary of $50,000.00 per year plus a $25,000.00 expense account. He was tired and continually unhappy that he didn't get out when the stock was high.

I made a proposition to him that delighted him. I told him that I would give him $200,000.00 cash for his controlling stock (100,000 shares) if he would agree to the following plan:

He was to hire me and present me to the board of directors as the new executive vice-president and his second in command. I was to receive a salary of $30,000.00 per year plus stock options.

When I was confirmed in my position (with the usual attendant publicity) I would then give him a cash down payment of $100,000.00 for one half of his stock. Then, after I had been aboard for three months and had thoroughly acquainted myself with the company, its operation and its personnel, he would announce that he was stepping out and naming me as the new chairman of the board (and controlling stock holder) whereupon I was to pay him the balance of $100,000.00 and receive the balance of the stock.

As soon as I had full control I called a special meeting of the board of directors and announced that instead of giving me the usual $50,000.00 salary and $25,000.00 expense account I was going to cut my salary to $10,000.00 per year and take shares of stock instead for the balance. This would free $65,000.00 in cash per year which I intended to use as bonus incentives for the workers and for an aggressive stockholder relations program.

Then I outlined a series of programs which included a Human Resources program designed to give the workers a forum for airing grievances; their own monthly newspaper, instituted a bowling program and gave them a new package of fringe benefits. This incidentally helped to eliminate the threat of a union strike which could have been disastrous at the time.

I brought in a new and aggressive Sales Representative organization which began to really boost sales to the point where we had to institute an ongoing recruitment program for additional workers.

All of these activities were fully publicized in a smooth public relations effort as well as a regular news letter to all stockholders (with copies to the investment analysts) and the end result was that active trading began and the stock began to rise.

When we issued a semi-annual report with a solid and factual forecast of increased earnings per share, things really began to move. I exercised my stock options (which permitted me to buy stock at the old price of 75¢ a share) and this, plus my 65,000 shares at the end of the year gave me a considerable holding in what was now a rapidly expanding public corporation, actively traded on the stock exchange.

A month before the preparation of our annual report a rumor hit the street that we were going to declare a dividend of more than a dollar a share for the first time in the company's history. Then things really began to hot up in the trading pits. I deposited thirty thousand shares of stock with my favorite stockbroker and gave him orders to sell slowly in stages above $10.00 per share. (You must file the necessary insider trading forms with the SEC.) I wanted them fed in slowly, not only to make the extra profits as the price rose, but to prevent a dumping effect.

I didn't have to be so cautious. The entire lot went in four days trading and the stock kept rising, but I was entirely satisfied. I still had more than enough cushion beyond my controlling shares to play with. All I wanted to do was to be able to return my investors $300,000.00.

Which I did, and then I also reaped the following:

The bank, after taking their $240,000.00 deposited $60,000.00 in my account plus my $30,000.00 interest on the bonds. I also had an added profit on the sale of my stock of $20,000.00.

So what did I gain for my original investment of $17,000.00 (which I borrowed from the bank)? I made $110,000.00 which was taxed as capital gains because it took a year to accomplish. I was chairman of the board of a successful publicly held corporation and also held the controlling shares of stock.

Sure I worked hard for it—an average of 12 hours a day for a full year. But it was certainly worth it. That operation started me on the road to becoming an actual millionaire. With that corporation as my base I began to acquire other companies.

The point is, that right from the beginning, I was using money—not spending it. And I was always aware that I was using other peoples' money. I always gave a better than usual return on the money and always saw to it that the original capital was returned intact.

This entire transaction, from beginning to end, was legal and legitimate. Everybody benefited from it. The fact that I received the biggest benefit is right and proper because I set it up and did all the work, everyone else just reaped without doing anything more than sowing the field with money.

Incidentally, the man I bought the company from was a really smart cookie. He took the money I gave him and quietly began buying stock and I'm not sure but I think he made the biggest killing of all—but that's fine. I'm glad he could. After all, he started the business from scratch and deserves to get the biggest reward.

Now, if you're sitting there saying to yourself.

"Well, sure. He had $30,000.00 to play with in the beginning. Where am I ever going to get that kind of money?" then please think about this, for a moment:

SIMPLE WAYS TO SAVE MONEY

I don't care how small your income is right now, if you want to save up a stake you can do it but you have to really cut out all frills and live a life of austerity for awhile. I'll bet, right now, you don't have the slightest idea of how much money you literally 'throw away' each day of your life. I really mean—throw it away.

Let me start to add up the waste that I began to eliminate from my life when I decided to get a stake:

Daily Burnups (I'll use today's prices)

Cigarettes	$ 2.80	(4 packs)
Coffee	1.40	(4 cups) (Before noon)
Buttered roll	.35	
Newspaper	.25	(Wall Street Journal)*
Lunch	2.00	(food)
Drinks	3.00	
Break Snack	.90	(Coffee and Bun)
Coffee	.70	(2 containers in the PM)
	11.40	

That's $57.00 per week!

(*) I took a company subscription
instead of buying in the stand.

I cut that figure drastically with the simple elimination of the cigarettes, the drinks and the coffee.

You can do it too. I'll show you how in the next chapter.

GETTING A GOOD CREDIT REPORT ON YOUR COMPANY

Incidentally, there is something you can do about getting a decent credit rating almost from the moment you open your office. Call the local office of Dun & Bradstreet and give them the kind of information you would want to be given out by them in case anyone checked your credit through Dun & Bradstreet. Naturally, since you are just beginning, there will be little you can tell them about your clients but you can give them details about the nature of your business, your personal background, credit references (use your attorney, accountant or any firm that has extended credit to you.

Don't worry about making your report sound like a press release. D & B reporters are very busy and they appreciate anything you can give them. Much of the actual language you employ will actually find its way into your credit file.

HOW TO MEET 100 SUCCESSFUL PEOPLE

One of the best ways to meet the people with money in your area is to join the local branch of the Rotary International. The membership is comprised of professional men (doctors, lawyers, architects, C.P.A.'s) as well as the chief executives of major firms and the owners of individual business firms. In other words, the financial elite in your area.

When you join the Rotary, you have an excellent opportunity to meet these men on an informal, first-name basis. You will, during the course of your membership, make many firm friendships as well as excellent business contacts.

If you take the time to become active in the affairs of the club you will advance up the ladder and can, in a relatively short time, become the president of your local branch. The reason is that most of the members prefer to be spectators and people who really hustle get elected to high posts quickly.

HOW TO GET SUPPLIER CREDIT

You will, from time to time, want to have an 'open account' with a supplier. One of the best ways to present your corporation in the best possible light, is to send a specially prepared presentation with your usual financial statement. It can be highly effective.

Quite recently one of our corporations diversified into retail sales of hardware, housewares, drugs and other retail products through leased departments in other company's stores.

We made a simple, typed presentation which helped us to obtain almost $1,000,000.00 in legitimate credit. This presentation talked about our concepts, executives and had the best credit references I could muster. Suppliers were impressed and most of them gave us credit.

GETTING FREE SERVICES FROM YOUR BANK

One of the simplest and easiest ways to obtain a credit check on any customer you intend to extend credit to is to check with the credit officer of your bank.

Quite recently we were considering leasing of space in two different stores. Both landlords seemed, on the surface to be substantial and successful. However the bank reports we received told an entirely different story.

Landlord "A", according to the report we received, had been a customer of the bank for nine years. He maintains a bank balance in the high 5 and low 6 figures. He honors all his commitments promptly. He has, from time to time, borrowed from the bank and was always on time with his loan repayments. The bank recommended him as an excellent businessman with character and integrity.

Landlord "B" was another matter. He was already in trouble with his mortgage payments; his bank account was overdrawn from time to time and the main reason why he wanted us to lease space in his store was to help to shore up his financial weakness and inability to meet his financial obligations.

This valuable and free credit check enabled us to bypass a loser and invest our money with a winner. Which is exactly what we did.

Remember this, the next time you need a quick and reliable credit report check with your banker. He can be a real friend.

He can be a friend in other ways, too. If you conduct your financial affairs with integrity and honor your obligations promptly you will favorably impress him. Many bankers are quite verbal and will speak up and give you a boost, if they feel you deserve it.

Another way you can benefit by making friends with your banker is the courtesy he will extend to you in the matter of drawing against deposited checks without making you wait three to five days (or longer). Of course, the legality of this may vary from state to state but where it is left to the discretion of the banker, you will derive interest-free use of large sums of money if your banker is friendly and well disposed towards you. So make friends with your banker.

HOW TO RAISE MONEY AND GET A GOOD EMPLOYEE

Another interesting way to acquire cash and, at the same time, acquire a top executive is to find an executive with cash who wanted ownership instead of just a position.

Recently, in one of my retail corporations I was searching for a really talented General Merchandising Manager. I was lucky enough to find a successful executive who was fed up with the never ending politics of the corporate world and also had $50,000.00 cash to invest.

Well, at one stroke, both of us solved our individual problems. He derived ownership in the corporation and I obtained an executive who really works because, in essence, he's working for himself. I also obtained additional cash which strengthened our position with banks and suppliers.

HOW TO RAISE MONEY, AND SAVE MONEY

Here's another variation on that same idea. Suppose, for example, you were a manufacturer and you needed additional capital. What you could do is to interest the various suppliers in becoming investors in your manufacturing company. Think of all the firms that supply you with material or services: the box companies, corrugated suppliers, printers, plastic companies, maintenance supplies, etc.

Each of those companies could invest in your company and insure that they would continue to be your major suppliers. You, on the other hand, would receive additional capital. It really works. And your new stockholders always give you their lowest prices.

HOW TO DEAL WITH YOUR DEBTS

Right about now you're probably saying, "It all sounds great for someone who has some money for a stake—but what about people like me? I'm in debt up to my ears!"

Relax. There is a solution to your debt problem—no matter how bad it may seem to you. The solution depends on exactly how bad your situation really is.

Let's take two, typical situations. You have an income of $14,000.00 a year and, because of a variety of events beyond your control, you are in debt to the tune of $12,000.00, and you're getting deeper into debt with each passing month.

There is one basic rule to follow whenever you owe substantial amounts of money. Don't wait for the creditors to call you. Call them first. Be honest with each creditor. Tell them that you're having a tough time right now but you have a chance to move into a decent job and will be able to start paying regularly but right now you need breathing space. You ask for a hiatus of about 60 days and thereafter you'll begin to make regular payments and will be able to clear up the debt in 90 to 120 days. That means 100% of the debt will be paid.

In today's society, every creditor would rather be paid slowly, even if it took a year, rather than wind up with nothing at all. Even if the creditor institutes a lawsuit he knows that legal and interest costs will eat up half his claim the day he turns it over to his attorney. And there's still no guarantee that he's going to get anything at all, if he takes that course.

As soon as you realize that you are going to be unable to pay your bills on a timely basis start calling your creditors.

If your creditors agree to your proposition you have—in essence, gained six months to spread your payments painlessly.

You may run into a creditor that won't go along with you. He just won't listen. He tells you that unless he receives his money within a specified time he's going to sue.

Then your only recourse is to beat him to the punch and sue him for invasion of privacy, undue harrassment, or whatever your attorney suggests. Let's suppose you owe the creditor about $4,000.00. Tell your attorney to institute a suit for 3 times that amount. That forces the creditor to counter-sue.

Which means that your suit has priority. Now with that long backlog in the courts which means considerable delay before your case gets on the court calendar—and the legal options of postponements and other delaying tactics, there is a strong possibility that long before the case ever comes to court, the creditor will try to make some kind of mutually beneficial settlement with you.

Naturally I do not advise an unethical or frivolous law suit, but if you have been harrassed, if you have received embarrassing or threatening phone calls, you have a right to sue.

Now there are some cases where people have gotten so far into debt that it's virtually impossible for them to ever pay back their debts. I remember the case of the charming couple who managed to get themselves deeply into debt ($50,000.00) even though their combined income was only $16,000.00.

It was perfectly clear that they couldn't possibly pay off their obligations within 6 months. So, upon the advice of their attorney, they filed under Chapter 13 of the Federal Bankruptcy Act.

Simply stated, this act allows you to erase all of your obligations by turning over the majority of your assets to your creditors. You should be represented by an attorney in this matter because there are several important technicalities that have to be considered.

One last thought before you seriously contemplate personal bankruptcy. There is a technique that will work in about 80% of all cases. Have your attorney write a letter to all of your creditors. The letter should state that the attorney has been retained to file a petition under Chapter 13 of the Federal Bankruptcy Act. He indicates, however, that his client is reluctant to do so, since he knows that his lack of significant assets will mean that the creditors will receive nothing.

The attorney's letter will then state that he has proposed an alternative plan to his client. He has suggested that his client (you) turn over 10% of his income each month, and the attorney will issue regular checks to all creditors each month, in proportion to each creditor's claim.

Even though this method might take several years to discharge all the debts, the creditors will be keenly aware that they will, eventually recover all of their money, which is a lot more sensible than permitting the filing of the petition for personal bankruptcy, which would mean they receive nothing.

The point of this essay on debt is to provide you with the realization that no matter how deeply you are in debt, solutions can be found which will actually solve your debt problems and permit you to explore the adventure of creating a second career and through it become able to live like a millionaire on an ordinary income.

In our next chapter we'll discuss the rare art of money management which, in addition to insuring that you do not get into debt again may put you on the road to becoming an actual millionaire instead of just living like one.

CHAPTER FIVE

THE ART OF MONEY MANAGEMENT

There isn't any mystery to the art of money management. It's just a matter of common sense. If you spend more money than you earn then you go into debt. If you spend less than you earn then you have money to save or invest. And these investments will help you to achieve your goal of living like a millionaire as soon as possible.

Perhaps if you started to think of your personal life as a business—and began to try to operate it as a business which you wanted to be profitable, it might be easier for you to grasp. Let's try it, for the moment and see how it works out. Let's pretend that I am going to 'buy' your personal life business from you.

The first thing that I'd want is a balance sheet—that's a sheet that shows your assets (everything you own) and your liabilities (how much you owe).

You add up the list of assets and write down the figure. Then you add up the list of liabilities and write down that figure. If the assets figure is larger than the liabilities figure than you have a 'net worth'—if the liabilities figure is larger than the assets figure then you have a 'net indebtedness'. It's that simple. If this seems very unsophisticated, ask yourself when was the last time you actually compiled your personal net worth.

Here's how you do it. Your first item is actual cash. You want to find out exactly how much cash you have right now. First empty your pockets. If you're married then have your partner do the same. Round up every penny from wallets, pocketbooks, cookie jar—the works. Next—add it all up and write down the figure. Now get your checkbooks and bank passbooks. Add up the balances. Any life insurance? Put down the cash value if you cashed them in tomorrow. Any stocks and bonds? How much would you get if you cashed them in tomorrow? Write that figure down. How many cars do you have? How much would you get if you sold them tomorrow? Use the trade-in value as an estimate. How about your house? How much could you get for it? Your furnishings? Any jewelry? Figure that you'd get about half its worth if you sold it tomorrow. Do you own a camper, boat, sports equipment? Add everything up.

Now you have to start adding up your liabilities.
1. Current debt?
2. How much is the balance of the mortgage?
3. Any car loans? (Total owed balance)
4. Personal loans? (Total owed balance)
5. Installment payments? (Owed balance)

Add up the figures. The difference is either your net worth (desirable) or your net indebtedness (undesirable).

Now we're going to consider your 'cash flow' (which is the money you receive each week) against your expenses. We'll do this first on a yearly basis. Just put down the amount on your weekly paycheck and multiply it by 52. This is your total income for your 'business' (unless you have income from other sources—add them to it).

Let's suppose that your total income for the year is $12,000. That means you cannot spend more than $1,000 per month without going into debt.

Now let's add up all your expenses for the year. That means everything. Mortgage (or rent), real estate taxes, school taxes, heat, gas, electric, telephone, insurance payments, tuition costs, pension or union dues, food, clothing, car maintenance or repair, recreation, gifts, magazine subscriptions, everything. Don't forget payments on loans, installments, etc.

Add it all up, divide it by 12 and if the amount per month is greater than $1,000. you're in trouble.

The answer is not borrowing—but cutting costs. Now there are some kinds of expenses which are fixed and can't be cut—like mortgage payments, real estate and school taxes, installment payments, loan payments and so forth.

On the other hand there are many expenses that can be cut down or eliminated for a period of time. If your balance sheet shows that you are going into debt each month then you have no choice but to set up a real 'austerity' program and cut some of your costs.

It needn't be forever—just for a certain period of time—say six months. During that period you will be ruthless in cutting out the non-essentials. That means anything that is not absolutely necessary.

Recreation: This has to be one of the largest non-essential costs. Just add up the expense entailed in going to a movie or a restaurant, once a week and then multiply that figure by 52. I'd be willing to bet, if you added it up correctly, that it would total more than $1,000.00 per year. That's a lot of money.

Deposit $15.00 (a modest sum) in your savings account each week for 26 weeks. Total: $450.00 plus interest.

Barber/Beautician: If you've been keeping track of your expenses you know exactly how much you spend per month. If you can cut the visits in half—how much would you save? Let's deposit $5.00 per week in the savings account for 26 weeks. Total: $150.00 plus interest.

Luxury Food: This is any kind of food or drink that is not essential to health or nutrition. Cake, cookies, candy, soft drinks, beer, wine, liquor, etc. Let's take another modest sum of $15.00 per week (which is much less than you actually spend) and deposit it in your savings account for 26 weeks. Total: $450.00 plus interest.

Daily Expenses: Again, if you've kept track of your daily expenses you should be shocked at the amount you spend each day for lunches, occasional cups of coffee at luncheonettes, occasional packs of cigarettes, a bar of candy or a package of chewing gum. Take lunches from home Monday, Wednesdays and Fridays. Eliminate all the unnecessary expenses. Deposit $10.00 a week in your savings account for 26 weeks. Total: $260.00 plus interest.

With just those four items we have mentioned you will have, in your savings account, at the end of six months, the sum of $1,310.00 plus interest. If you keep that austerity program going for a year, you will have the sum of $2,620.00 plus interest in your savings account.

The odd part about it is, that once you start eliminating the non-essential, you really don't miss them but you sure do appreciate watching your bank account grow larger.

There isn't any magic in money management. It merely requires that you be fully conscious of every penny you spend.

Just remember, every penny you spend vanishes. Every penny you save, begins to earn money with every tick of the clock.

There are many other ways to save money easily. Food shopping, according to the economists, takes one third of your income. That's a mighty big chunk. Is there a way to save money when you shop for food (other than by eliminating the non-essentials as we discussed)?

Yes. You can do it the same way a business does when it buys essential supplies. They use a Stock Keeping Unit method (SKU) which simply means that they keep an inventory on the supplies they use over a period of a year. They know exactly how much they use of each item during the period of a year. Do you know? Then you'd better start examining it. Let's suppose, for the sake of an example, that you discover that your family uses two cans of string beans a week. That's one hundred and four cans a year. Whenever you see a 'special sale' on string beans stock up—buy a couple of dozen cans (if there's no limit) and make a note of the money you've saved.

Use your SKU concept to keep a running inventory of the items on hand—relative to your year-long need—and stock up each time there's a 'special sale'. Each time you do, put the cash savings in a jar or a can. Watch those savings start to mount up.

If you have a freezer you can use the SKU method to plan your meat and poultry purchases in bulk and save a considerable sum over the year.

Read your daily paper carefully—watch for savings coupons or 'loss leader' sales items which stores offer to entice you to shop on certain days. There's no need to buy anything but the loss leaders. It's legitimate. The storekeeper hopes you'll buy something else while you're there but there is no obligation on your part.

You can use the SKU method when you make major purchases for items like clothing. You should have a good idea of the basic need—the items on hand—the amount of clothing you purchase during the year. Then shop for clothing during the 'sales events' which are usually seasonal and offer up to 50% off regular prices. There's a list, at the end of this chapter, of all the sales events which take place from January through December. Use that list to mark your calendar with the events right through the year. Then when you turn your calendar pages you'll have an immediate reminder. Try to shop for your children's clothes a year in advance for the greatest savings. Buy their winter clothing during the Spring Clearance and their summer clothes at the end of summer. Always remember to buy a size larger (they do grow, you know).

When you decide to buy any major appliance—stoves, washing machines, dishwashers, television sets—buy them during the special sales events. Read your Consumer Reports for "Best Buys"—shop around and get competitive bids just the way a business firm does.

When you're ready to buy that major appliance do not buy it on the installment plan. It can cost you from 18% up in interest and service charges. Do not pay cash. (Remember you use money—instead of spending it.)

Take a passbook loan at your savings bank. Interest charges are about 2½%. Then make regular payments to your account until you've paid it off. Pretend that you actually bought it on the installment plan. Let's say your major purchase cost $600.00 with 18% added for interest. You pay yourself back at the rate of $60.00 per month (approximately $15.00 per week). This means that at the end of the year you have paid yourself back $720.00.

Now if you had actually taken out that installment loan your cost for interest would have been $108.00. That means at the end of the year you would have paid off the loan and had $12.00 left.

But because you took out a passbook loan your interest charge was only $15.00 for the year. That's a total of $615.00. When you make your last payment you have paid off your loan and now have, in the bank, the sum of $105.00 plus your original $600. which you borrowed still intact.

See the difference?

You never disturb your capital. It just continues to grow. As it grows you have more and more 'borrowing power'—which is the ability to issue yourself a 'passbook loan' up to 90% of your savings in about 15 minutes with no questions asked.

Use the same technique when you decide to buy a new car. First you check out the best buys in Consumer Reports— they're available at your local library. Then you buy your car during the end of the year clearance (when the new models are about to appear). You can drive a really hard bargain because car dealers have to get rid of those cars. If they don't they'll have to wholesale them and take a real bath.

So be sharp in bargaining.

Remember you do not buy on the installment plan. You do not spend your cash. If possible, you take a passbook loan and pay yourself back at the same rate you'd pay back the installment loan. Remember to add on 18% for 3 years. On a $4,000.00 purchase that comes to $720.00 more. On your passbook loan it only costs you $100.00 more. That's quite a difference, isn't it? Plus the fact that at the end of three years you have your car and your money plus the difference between $720.00 and $100.00.

It certainly pays to be your own best friend at your savings bank. When you make a passbook loan there is no urgency in paying it back (but you should do it regularly just as though you had an installment loan).

However, if an emergency should arise and you were forced to miss a payment or two—there would be no penalty of any kind. Or, if you wished to stretch your payments over four or five years—that would be up to you also. You are in complete charge of your payback method. Which can be a comforting feeling in time of need or emergency.

Just remember—whenever you're tempted to 'spend' money, for any reason—stop and think. If I spend it—it's gone—if I use it—I never really let it go. And that's the way to financial independence. In business or in personal life, the goal is to build your capital (your savings) to a point of complete independence and freedom from financial worries.

It can be done—you know that now.

Now let's discuss the various types of stores and how they operate with regard to 'mark up' which is the percentage they charge above the wholesale price of an item like clothing, furniture and appliances.

There are four major categories. We'll discuss each of them in turn relative to your desire to save money whenever you purchase any major item like clothing, furniture, appliances, television sets, etc.

First of all there are the most expensive shops:

SPECIALTY SHOPS: 40% to 50% PROFIT MARK-UP (and higher)

These are usually run by smart (and charming) people who specialize in a particular type of merchandise. Whatever they have to offer you can bet it's 'top of the line' and of course the items are high priced. They justify this by offering considerable service. You are given a lot of assistance in buying and they also service what they sell. They back all their merchandise personally, in most cases, which means if you have a complaint they will make it good (generally) quickly and efficiently. When the specialty is clothing—you can get very good buys when they have clearance sales—as much as 50% off and sometimes it pays to buy as long as you remember that with 50% off at these shops you're still paying as much as 25% above wholesale. For the present you should avoid these shops.

DEPARTMENT STORES: 33% to 40% MARK-UP (and higher)

There is something fascinating about a department store, particularly the top stores. They spend a considerable amount of time and money to delight your eye and whet your appetite. When you enter a department store be careful. You can become almost hypnotized by the clever displays. A great deal of thought and psychology goes into the way they present merchandise. The longer you stay, the more chance there is that you'll buy something besides what you came into the store to buy.

If there is something you want—if it's on special sale—go directly to the department—buy the item and then leave quickly before you fall under the spell and start buying things you don't really need.

Remember too—if there's a clearance sale of 50% that can mean you're still paying from 16% to 20% above wholesale price. Do not be dazzled by the difference between the 'regular' price and the sale price. Shop around before you buy. Get competitive bids. That's particularly true if it's a nationally advertised item. There is a certain amount of service (it varies from store to store) and, in general, the department store will stand behind its merchandise and make replacement.

DISCOUNT STORES: 20% to 30% MARK-UP (sometimes higher)

The 'discount stores', particularly the chains of discount

stores, are usually able—through large purchasing power—to make 'better' buys on nationally advertised merchandise. However there are cases where the manufacturer has produced two types of products—a department store model and a discount store model. Be sure of the item before you buy. Also be careful of the smooth talking discount store salesman who will try to talk you 'up' to a higher priced item than the one that was advertised. It's called 'bait and switch' which means the store will advertise a nationally advertised product as a 'loss leader' to get you to come into the store. Then the smooth talking salesman will 'knock' the loss leader and try to show you something 'better' for only a few dollars more.

If ever you should encounter this pitch—leave the store immediately—report the tactic to your consumer advocate council. Because that tactic is not only unethical it's also illegal.

If you should insist on the loss leader and they tell you they're 'sold out' and it's still very early—report that too. That's as illegal as bait and switch. The store must advertise the exact number of items if they're low.

Don't expect service or delivery from a discount store. You generally have to take the item with you. If anything goes wrong—don't go back to the discount store—get in touch with the manufacturer. Discount stores are often not particularly interested in service or warranty problems. They refer you to the manufacturer.

CATALOG STORES: 15% to 20% MARK-UP (maybe higher)

This is a relatively new phenomenon. This is the least costly way to buy brand name items. You must know in advance exactly what you want. There is little or no display. You check out the catalog in the store—write up your own ticket—take it to a clerk who sends back to the warehouse and the item (in a carton) is brought up to you. You pay for it and take it with you. If something goes wrong you can (in some cases) bring it back and they'll make good (sometimes). It's a good idea to ask about their refund or replacement policy before you purchase.

Just remember that you are completely on your own at a catalog store. Expect very little help. You have to know what you want before you go. Then, check the catalog—the model number—color—accessories and final price (plus tax) and write up your slip.

Not fancy but you can save money.

If you really put your mind to saving money, you can do it quite easily. You simply have to gain complete control of your spending habits. It means you have to be fully conscious of every penny that you spend. Here's a really simple way—with a 15¢ investment—that you can produce a perfect picture of your daily spending habits.

Buy a little, 15¢ notebook, and for one solid week, write down every penny that you spend. For example if you stop and buy a newspaper in the morning—mark it down: Newspaper 15¢.

If you stop at the luncheonette for a cup of coffee, mark it down: Coffee 35¢. If you go out to lunch at noon—mark it down:

> Lunch $2.50, tip 25¢. Package of cigarettes: 70¢;
> Cigar: 25¢ etc.

At the end of the week add up everything you've spent. We'll call that sum 'out-of-pocket' expenses. Let's say $25.00.

Now, on Monday morning, before you leave the house, you will place a $5.00 bill in your right hand pocket (or left hand pocket if you're left handed) and $20.00 in the other pocket. You will continue to write down your expenses. However, you will begin to vary your buying habits.

When you start to buy the newspaper—stop and say: Do I really need it? When you start towards the luncheonette stop and say: Do I really need that cup of coffee? The answer is: No. You're better off without it. Eliminate the cup of coffee. When you decide to buy that pack of cigarettes ask yourself: Is it wise to pay 70¢ for a pack of cigarettes when I can buy a carton for $5.00? The answer is: No. If you just can't do without that 70¢ pack of cigarettes then try to make it go twice as far by smoking every 'other' cigarette. That is—each time you reach for a cigarette tell yourself that you will 'skip this one' and wait a half hour until you smoke the next one. If you start that kind of rationing you'll find that you not only save money—you'll be healthier as well. If you make that pack of cigarettes last for two days instead of one—you can put 70¢ aside every other day. When you have enough to buy a carton you will have reduced your cost to 50¢ a pack. Then, if you continue with your every 'other' cigarette and stretch that pack to two days you can begin putting away 50¢ every other day. That way—

each time you run out of cigarettes you'll have your $5.00 for a new carton. It can't hurt to try it.

Now at the end of each day (just before you go to bed) empty out your jacket pockets—or your pocket book—change purse—(or that right hand pocket where you put the $5.00) and take whatever's there in change and put it in a jar or can.

At the end of the week, take some coin wrappers and roll up all the pennies, nickels, dimes and quarters (if you have any change left over put it back in the jar). Add this sum to your regular weekly deposit. Not only will it make your capital grow—it will increase the amount of interest you receive. Which is money earning money with every tick of the clock.

Now let's discuss something called 'limited objective savings' which simply means that you will be saving money for a certain length of time for a specific item. Let's suppose that it's a television set. A good, color television set. We set an objective price of $600.00. Now how are we going to save this money? Not out of the household money—that's not fair. Well—the only other source of money is your $25.00 out-of-pocket expense money. Could you save enough out of that? Let's suppose that you took $10.00 and left yourself $15.00—that means you would only have $3.00 per day for spending money. Could you get by on that? If you can, then you'd have $520.00 plus interest in one year.

Too long to wait? Well, you could put twenty dollars a week away—of course that only leaves you a dollar a day for spending money. Could you get by with that amount? If you can—then you've got your set in about six months.

Just remember—you do not withdraw the cash you take a passbook loan because we never spend our capital—we use it— over and over to make more money.

Incidentally—if you already have a passbook loan that doesn't mean you can't increase the size of your loan, as long as you have a remainder in your account. You can borrow up to 90% of your savings account but don't do that. Never take more than 80%. That way you'll always have a little cushion.

Just remember that your savings are being deposited each week so that your equity in your capital is constantly increasing (and so is your earned interest.)

So after you have saved your 'extra' money for the television set there will be no problem in increasing your passbook loan. You'll have the cash in your hand in less than fifteen minutes.

However, you must pay back that 'extra' loan amount. You can do that quite easily. Take $10.00 a week from your weekly 'expense' money and you'll have the loan paid back in a year.

If you keep doing this kind of saving and borrowing (and pay back regularly) you will never be in debt again and you'll wind up with a substantial bank account.

Here are some more tips on how to save money:

Don't drive—walk: When you have to pick up a few items from the store, leave the car home and walk to the store and back. In addition to saving you gas, it will also help to improve your health.

Shovel your own snow: Don't pay somebody to shovel your walk or your driveway. Do it yourself—in easy stages—and put the money in your jar for savings. The exercise will do you good.

Wash—don't dry clean: Whenever possible, buy clothes that are 'wash and wear'. You'll be amazed at how much money you'll save when you eliminate dry cleaning. Put the money you save, each time, in your savings jar.

Eliminate Magazines: Let some of your magazine subscriptions lapse and do not renew for at least a year. Put the money for the subscriptions in your savings jar.

Cancel your book club: Do you realize that you can save at least $5.00 a month if you cancel your book club membership? Put the money you save, each month, in your saving jar. If any member of your family gives you any flack about the books or magazines—remind them that there is a public library that permits you to read books and magazines on or off the premises.

Eliminate Paper Napkins: Buy yourself some cloth napkins. Buy three sets, one for each member of the family. At the end of each day throw the soiled napkins in the washing machine along with the towels and wash cloths. Take the money you save and put it in your jar.

Eliminate Rolls of Paper Towels: Buy handiwipes. Each handiwipe lasts longer than a paper towel roll, at a fraction of the cost. Put the savings, etc.

Bake Your Own Bread: With the cost of bread today and the way your family uses it, you'd save a bundle by baking your own. It's a lot of fun and more nutritious!

Make Your Own Milk: Milk is another outrageously

overpriced item. Buy non-fat dry milk and mix your own. You'll also save money. Put the savings away.

Turn Down the Thermostat: Keep your house on the cool side during the winter—65 degrees in the daytime and 60 degrees at night when you go to bed. Your family will be healthier and you'll save on your fuel bills.

Cold Water Wash: You'll save fuel if you do your laundry in cold water. You'll get just as clean a wash but at a much lower cost.

Sew Your Own: If you're handy with a needle and thread your children can be dressed better and at lower cost. So can you. If you really become expert you can start wearing outfits that could cost up to a hundred dollars for as little as $20.00.

Wash Your Own Car: Stop taking your car to the car wash. Do it yourself with the garden hose. Put the money you save in your savings jar.

Change Your Own Oil: Buy motor oil at automotive stores whenever they have a special sale. Get 30 or 40 cans at a time. You'll save plenty each time you add oil—and a lot more when you change it. Remember to buy a new filter when you change it. Use the gallon size, plastic milk containers to catch the old oil. Put them out with the garbage.

Try 'rationing' your cigarettes. Here's how. Figure out how many packs of cigarettes you smoke in a week. Buy two or three cartons of cigarettes (at a discount store) at about $5.00 a carton, including tax, you will have invested $15.00.

Now try this technique. Ration yourself to one cigarette in a half hour. That means, in an eight hour day you will only be permitted 16 cigarettes. If you should forget and not smoke one a half hour later you cannot double up in the next half hour. You still can only have one cigarette and must wait a half hour for the next one. Try this for a week and then make the rule of only one cigarette in any hour. That means you must wait for one full hour after smoking a cigarette before you light the next one. Do that for a week and then cut the cigarettes to one every two hours.

By the third week you can reduce it to one cigarette every three hours and very shortly after that you will find that you can actually stop smoking entirely and then look at the money you'll save!

The main thing to be aware of is that you can have a really enjoyable life without things you now think are indispensible.

YOUR CHECKLIST FOR SALES EVENTS

JANUARY: This is a big month for sales, especially the first few weeks (after Christmas). January White Sales is also featured which means bedding, linen, towels, washcloths, bathmats, etc., all at reduced prices.

FEBRUARY: Most stores hold their final clearance on winter items in February. There are sales on furniture, bedding, floorcovering, washer/dryers, housewares and dishes. Washington's Birthday & Lincoln's Birthday Sales are also big events.

MARCH: This is the month for sales on ski equipment and ice sakes, luggage, hosiery and reduced prices on boys' and girls' shoes.

APRIL: Easter/Passover and Spring Sales all over.

MAY: Blankets, linens, handbags, lingerie & Memorial Day sales.

JUNE: Sales on dairy products and frozen foods, sportswear and outdoor furniture, floor coverings, building materials, lumber and tire sales, (after Father's Day)—men's wear sales.

JULY: Summer clothing, bathing suits, sportswear, sporting goods, storm windows, outdoor games and stereo.

AUGUST: Car dealers start pushing out their end-of-the-year models to make way for the new models coming in. You can bargain sharply for the car you want.

Most stores do their absolutely final sales on summer clothing and summer items like fans, outdoor equipment, outdoor furniture, bathing suits.

SEPTEMBER: You'll find sales on freezers, china, glassware, housewares, paints and home improvement materials. End-of-the-year car sales are still going on. Sales on mufflers and car batteries. This is also the month to buy season tickets for cultural events. Labor Day Sales are big events in many areas.

OCTOBER: Columbus Day, Thanksgiving and Veteran's Day are all sales events.

NOVEMBER: There aren't too many sales because the Christmas shopping is underway. However there may be Election Day Sales in some areas.

DECEMBER: This is the worst month to shop for bargains except for the week after Christmas and even then it would be better to wait until the first week in January. Never do your Christmas shopping in December—do your shopping all year long and get great presents at real savings during the sales event.

Remember, if you can plan your major purchases a year in advance you can take advantage of many of the great sales events that take place during the year and really save money.

Incidentally, if you have to buy a new car, there is a firm that can help you to bargain very closely with any new car agency. For example, when you look at a new car there's a sticker sheet on the window which tells you exactly what the car costs and the cost of all the individual accessories. Wouldn't it be nice if you knew exactly what that had cost the dealer? You'd know exactly how much profit he was playing with and you could strike a pretty good bargain (within reason). He wouldn't stay in business long if he didn't make some profit. You can just make sure that he doesn't make too much profit on you.

Here's what you do. Check out the make, model and year of the car you really want, then send that information to an outfit called Car/Puter, 1603 Bushwick Avenue, Brooklyn, N.Y. 11207. The fee is $10.00. They'll send you back a computer readout which gives the dealer price as well as the retail price. With that information you can really do some tough bargaining for the car you want.

Just remember—whatever you do—try not to spend money unnecessarily—and always, if possible—use money rather than spend it.

In our next chapter we're going to talk about the pros and cons of a college education.

CHAPTER SIX

OBTAINING A VALID COLLEGE DEGREE WITHOUT ATTENDING A COLLEGE OR UNIVERSITY

One of the most damaging concepts in modern business practice is the myth that a man or woman who does not have a valid college degree is inferior to a person who does.

It's damaging to business and industry because year after year, perfectly intelligent and fully capable men and women are not even considered for executive positions because they lack a degree. These competent men and women have to sit by and watch a nincompoop with a degree fumble with a position and, in many cases, have to support the misfit in order to keep their department functioning.

The strange part is, that virtually anyone can get a perfectly valid, fully acceptable degree without attending college (in person) and without spending thousands of dollars doing it. There are a number of excellent colleges and universities throughout the United States that offer external degree programs. Some of them require that you spend a certain amount of time on campus—others only require that you take a final examination for your degree either at the college or university—or—if you prefer, a location near your home.

Before we get into the deeper explanation of these programs there's something else for you to consider.

There is a special program that's vitally important to you if you are seriously intending to seek a degree. It's called the College Level Examination Program (CLEP). The idea is that it makes it possible for anybody to earn up to two years of college credit by taking a series of weekend tests. Thousands of colleges and universities all over the nation now recognize the validity of these examinations and will give you up to two years credit when you enroll.

The reasoning behind this program is quite sound. The people who founded it believe that you didn't stop learning after you left high school. If you are the type of person that reads a lot, keeps up with current events, attends various cultural events or possibly watched the educational programs on television, you have learned a great deal. You may have taken courses in adult education programs, or even non-credit courses at a community college. Whatever you did, you learned and the CLEP program is a way of turning that learning into college degree credits.

If this program interests you (and it should) then write to:

College Level Examination Program
P.O. Box 592, Princeton, New Jersey 08540
Att: Publications Order Office.
Ask for their CLEP Booklet, which is free of charge.

· The booklet will give you a description of the kind of examinations you can expect, a list of the schools which use and accept the program and information about the location of test centers where you may take the actual examinations.

The cost is about $15.00 for a general examination and $15.00 per subject examination. It's well worth the money when you consider how much two years' college credits would cost you today.

Naturally, once you have up to two years credits under your belt it's a much shorter way to go to get the full degree. However, with or without those credits you can enroll in a lot of fine universities and colleges around the country who have instituted external degree programs. These are, in essence, correspondence courses which you do at home. The college sends you the assigned lessons and homework which you prepare and mail back to them. They send back the corrected and graded papers. When you complete the work in a particular subject you must sit for a supervised examination, either at the college or university that you are working with or at a designated place with a qualified proctor. That's the way most of them operate.

Some colleges, like Goddard College, Plainfield, Vermont 05667, have an 18 month Bachelor of Arts degree program which requires that you alternate two weeks on campus with six months of home study. The degree is well thought of and will permit you to take graduate studies for your Masters or Ph.D. It costs about $3,000.00 and you have to pay for your own accommodations while on campus (plus travel).

If you prefer the university correspondence courses then you can obtain more information by writing to:

The National University Extension Association
Suite 360
One DuPont Circle
Washington, D.C. 20036
Ask for: The Guide to Independent Study through
Correspondence Instruction

It costs 50¢ and lists all the universities in the program, their addresses and the hundreds of courses they offer. Here are some of the top schools in the program:

Independent Study ·
University of California
Berkeley, Cal. 94720

Independent Study
University of Kansas
Lawrence, Kansas 66044

Independent Study
University Extension Div.
University of Nebraska
Lincoln, Nebraska 65808

College of Continuing
    Education
University of Oklahoma
Norman, Oklahoma 73069

University Extension
University of Kentucky
Lexington, Kentucky 40506

Correspondence Study
Owen Hall
Indiana University
Bloomington, Indiana 47401

Independent Study
227 Extension Building
University of Wisconsin
Madison, Wisconsin 53706

Independent Study
Office of Continuing Education
State University of New York
30 Russell Road
Albany, New York 12206

Correspondence Study
3 Shields Building
Pennsylvania State University
University Park,
Pennsylvania 16902

There are, of course, other correspondence schools like ICS
(International Correspondence Schools) and LaSalle which
have been around for many generations. Actually there are
something like 180 different private correspondence schools
around the country. If you would like a free directory of all
these schools write to: National Home Study Council
                        1601 Eighteenth Street
                        Washington, D.C. 20009
Ask for:
Directory of Accredited Private Home Study Schools.

The categories I have given you are the best. However there
are a certain number of other colleges which must be termed
'borderline' because although they give you a 'legal' degree for
home study work, it is not a respected degree. Also, for the
most part, you cannot do graduate work with them because
they are not really accredited colleges. That means if you
obtained a Bachelor's degree at one of the borderline colleges
and then wanted to go to a decent college for graduate work
you would not be able to.

If you don't care about graduate work and just want a degree
that's 'legal' but not respected, by all means pick one of those
borderline colleges. The degree will cost several hundred
dollars. You can find them through advertisements in a wide

126

range of magazines, many of the magazines being quite respectable, some not so respectable. I'm not going to name the colleges because there are libel laws and I don't want to get into a legal hassle about whether they are or are not 'borderline'.

If you care about your degree and you find a college and want to know whether or not it's fully accredited then here are the places around the country that you can write to and find out exactly what the college status is:

Middle States Association of Colleges
225 Broadway, New York, N.Y. 10007

New England Association of Colleges
50 Beacon Street, Boston, Mass. 02108

North Central Association of Colleges
5454 South Shore Drive, Chicago, Ill. 60615

Northwestern Assoc. of Secondary & Higher Schools
3731 University Way, Seattle, Wash. 98105

Southern Association of Colleges & Universities
795 Peachtree Street, NE, Atlanta, Georgia 30308

Western Association of Schools and Colleges
c/o Mills College, Oakland, California 94613

Finally, of course, we come to the diploma 'mills' which are, for the most part, nothing more than printing plants that turn out worthless diplomas for whatever the traffic will bear. The price can range from a low of $25.00 to a high of $500.00, although why anyone in his right mind would pay that much money for a fake diploma is beyond me.

Consider two basic facts about a fake diploma. If you apply for a job with one you are committing a legally wrong act by making a false statement. Even if you should get the job and they check it out later you would be fired under rather grim circumstances. If you weren't found out you would be uncomfortable because you would know that at some time or another the truth would come out.

However, if you don't really care, and just want something to hang on the wall to impress people with, go ahead. You'll find these kinds of diploma mills advertising in all sorts of magazines such as the kind you find in beauty parlors and barber shops. You'll also find their ads in national weekly newspapers like The Star, Inquirer and Moneysworth.

If you're wondering how they can get away with it, then let me explain about it. Would you like to open your own college or university for less than $100.00? You can, in most of these United States because of the laws that insure religious freedom throughout our nation.

Now let me add, at this point, that there are a number of very fine, fully accredited religious colleges and universities in this country and they are by no means to be considered as diploma 'mills' turning out worthless diplomas. They are not the ones I'm talking about.

You see, all you have to do to open a religious college or university is to file a certificate of incorporation of a non-profit organization with the Secretary of State (in the state where the school or college will be built.)

Once your non-profit corporation is established you then file an application with the Internal Revenue Service and the Treasury Department of the United States. If, after examining your application, there is nothing wrong with it (your background is clear of criminal record, etc.) these agencies will grant you an exemption from Federal Income Tax. That goes further—if your home should be 'owned' by the religious college you have founded, it too may be tax free. That means all taxes, property taxes and school taxes—everything! So you can begin to understand why these colleges and universities start up in the first place. The diplomas are a secondary source of income. There's also a special ruling that any bequests, donations, gifts, etc. that are made by any sponsors to your college are tax free to you—but tax deductible to the donors.

Is the picture becoming clear? Well, it gets better as we go along. These religious colleges and universities, once founded, can offer special courses towards Bachelor of Arts, Science and Divinity. They all also offer Masters and Doctors degrees. Oddly enough, in some states, their Doctor of Divinity degree will permit you to practice as an ordained minister in certain churches. Which means that you can actually perform marriages, baptisms and other religious services so long as they comply with the law of that state, they are legal services.

Then, too, as a man of the cloth and an ordained minister you get preferential treatment from many organizations including special rates on some airlines.

Now, with all the warnings I've given you about the dangers

of a 'fake' diploma, if you want to go ahead—go and enjoy yourself. Just don't try to get a decent job with one of those fake diplomas—it means big trouble.

Last and by every means least—we come to the companies that offer blank diplomas—a sort of do-it-yourself diploma. You just fill in the name of the college or university and your own name and presto! you have a college degree. You can get two for a dollar.

You have to admit that the blank diploma is the simplest and cheapest way of the entire lot. Frankly it's worth exactly the same as a diploma mill product and costs a heck of a lot less. So if you just want to impress the neighbors and paper your wall— by all means buy the blank diploma.

You should, by the way, just for the fun of it, write to some of the diploma mills and obtain their brochures and pamphlets. I did, while we were doing research for this book and some of the material that came back was really funny.

There was one outfit (we naturally cannot mention the name) that sent a brochure advertising a Bachelor of Arts degree (with no home study—just a donation) for $55.00—a Master's Degree for a $75.00 donation and a Ph.D. for $100.00 donation. However—if we took all three, at once, we could have the lot for $150.00 which they pointed out was a clear savings of $75.00!

How could anyone refuse a bargain like that?

In all seriousness, if you want a valid degree you will have to work for it and pay for it. Look into the CLEP program and see if you can earn up to two years' credits by examination—that's well worth the effort.

Then pick the best college or university and then buckle down and go to work at earning your valid degree. Once you have it you can expect to move up the ladder and earn more money. It's been estimated that with only four years of high school behind you the average lifetime earnings you can expect would be $350,000.00 but with a four-year college degree behind you that figure goes up to $586,000. which is a lot higher in anyone's book.

Just remember—if you start—please make every effort to continue to the end.

In our next chapter we're going to delve into the world of public relations and show you some of the tricks of the trade that can be extremely useful to you.

West poses in his North Babylon warehouse with some of his firms' toys

...till working out the price struc-
...res for the ba·
...'s cousins or friends, and it wil
...thinking about hittin
...ple with the book by
...That's a reasonable n
...y beyond est or TM. A
...to join the Mind Spa
...atever is going to work
...e we're after."
...hat? "Th·

can't afford it? They can have it
and if it works for them they'll

'West's book asks you to reca
all your good experiences a
to exorcise all the bad.'

rhetoric since Charlton Heston came dow
mountain with the tablet in his hands. Bu
the least I could do was read the book. It divides
me to do, and reach some kind of eval
happens, the book ain't bad. It divides
chapters, one exercise a day for a mom
to be a prolonged exercise in autogene
in which you are asked to remembe
things in your life like the last time yo
or a zoo, and to exercise all the ba
life like fidgeting and procrastina
course, a great deal more to the
...kind, none of it harmfu
...n it works depen

CHAPTER SEVEN

HOW TO USE
PUBLICITY AND
PUBLIC RELATIONS

131

We're going to discuss Publicity and Public Relations at some length because this area of your overall plan is highly critical. Regardless of how successful you are with every other phase of this operation, if you mishandle P.R. (Public Relations) and/or publicity you can suffer a setback that can be extremely difficult to recover from.

Let's begin with some basic facts. Advertising and publicity are just two of the many different tools that P.R. professionals may use to achieve a particular objective.

The question then is: What exactly is P.R.?

Simply stated, P.R. can be described as the activities connected with interpreting and improving the relationship of an individual or an organization with the public.

To put it another way: P.R. is the art of controlling an enhancing the image of a client's public behavior.

You see, a P.R. specialist must function at a policy-making level and thus provide advice and counsel to the individual or organization. The objective is to insure that the individual or organization does not engage in activities that can create an unfavorable public image.

Since you will, for the foreseeable future at least, be acting as your own P.R. man it's essential that you fully understand the fundamentals of P.R. and thus avoid some of the pitfalls that lie in wait for the untutored and unwary.

That same understanding, when you do finally hire a P.R. man, will help you to assess his performance and capabilities. So pay attention. It's important.

Let's examine some of the things that P.R. can and cannot do. For example: When Ivy Ledbetter Lee, who has been called 'the father of P.R. in America' was engaged by the original John D. Rockefeller and entrusted with the task of changing Rockefeller's bad public image he informed his client that it could not be done unless Rockefeller's public behavior changed. When John D. Rockefeller actually became a true, public benefactor and philanthropist then Ivy Lee, through a carefully calculated P.R. program succeeded in changing Rockefeller's public image.

This brings us to the First Law of Public Relations.

P.R. cannot change sow's ears into silk purses.

The way you walk, talk, dress and interact with people is an essential part of your public image. If you do it well then P.R.

can operate effectively on your behalf. Do it badly and no amount of P.R. can change that image.

Now, perhaps, you can realize the significance of being aware, at all times, that you are 'on stage'; that you are being observed and judged by your actions.

Let's pretend, for the moment, that you have hired a P.R. professional. We will also assume that you have established your furnished, corporate headquarters and that your P.R. man is seated opposite you and says:

"All right, Mr. Jones. What can I do for you?"

What would you say to him? Now think about that for a moment. There he is, ready and waiting for you to tell him exactly what you want him to do—and, to be perfectly honest, you really don't know what to say to him. This brings us to the Second Law of P.R.

You must have a clearly defined goal or objective in mind before you launch any P.R. campaign.

After listening to this piece of advice offered by your P.R. man, you do some heavy thinking and finally say:

"I guess I want to be famous—or well known, at least."

Your P.R. man waits courteously for you to continue and when it's obvious that you have said your piece, he asks,

"Famous for what?"

It's a perfectly valid question that brings us to:

The Third Law of P.R.

You must have a clearly defined, realistic image in mind before you launch any P.R. campaign.

Again, that's logical. You cannot expect your P.R. man to make you famous as a brain surgeon if you can't put a band-aid on your thumb without assistance.

So you think about it and then say:

"I'd like to become well known as the chief executive of a successful corporation. Is that possible?"

"It's quite possible, Mr. Jones. Well known to whom?"

That's a reasonable question. Unless you intend to run for the office of President of these United States and had several million dollars to play with, there is little reason for you to convince the entire world that you are an 'up and coming' chief executive. Thus we have:

The Fourth Law of P.R.

You must have a clearly defined 'target audience' in mind before you launch any P.R. campaign.

You think about that and then say:

"I want to become well known to bankers, business men and luxury car dealers within a 100 mile radius of my office. How's that?"

"That's fine, Mr. Jones. Now tell me something about yourself and your corporation."

Now there you are. What should you tell him? You really have to think about it. This brings us to:

The Fifth Law of P.R.

You must be as honest with your P.R. man as you are with your lawyer or doctor. A professional P.R. man is bound by the same seal of silence with respect to all confidences he may receive in the course of his work.

You must also be just as honest with yourself.

To do that you should recognize one fact: what you are trying to do is neither dishonest or illegal. You are in all cases, trading a talent for 'things' or for money. You will be using P.R. to create a good reputation and enhance your public image. There is nothing wrong with that. The fact is that while you are—in the main—creating an illusion—that illusion is really turning into fact.

Consider the following facts:

1. You are the chief executive of a corporation.
2. The corporation does exist in conformity with law.
3. You do have furnished corporate headquarters.
4. You are empowered as the renting agent and manager.
5. You do have a contractual agreement with the office-furniture leasing corporation.
6. You can offer a viable 'furnished office leasing' concept with added benefits to the tenant.
7. You do have legal and tax consultant associates at your corporate headquarters.
8. You will offer your unique services to other office building owners in the near future.

These facts can be used as the basis for one or several Press Releases. If they were professionally written to convince a news editor that they were 'newsworthy'—which means they would be of interest to the reader—then there is every chance that they will be included in the paper as a brief or lengthy news story— depending on the space that was available to the editor.

Photography could also be employed. For example: a

picture of a vacant office side-by-side with the same office fully furnished with a picture caption describing the many tax advantages offered by the 'totally leased' office and the elimination of the need for large, initial, capital expense.

Your own 'formal' portrait, with a picture caption describing you as the chief executive of the corporation and your 'total lease' concept which you hope to promote in other office buildings, could also be disseminated.

Using the basic facts about your legal and tax expert associates (brief biographies, etc.) you could send out a corporate release which might be picked up as a business news column 'brief' by the business news editor. You could also incorporate the facts about your associates in a general news release which dealt with the unusual services your corporation offered to prospective tenants.

In either case you would strengthen the relationship with your two professional associates (this too is public relations) and could expect greater loyalty from them.

The overall impact, within your target area, of this kind of public relations campaign is much greater than you realize. While it is true that you are rapidly creating a powerful personal public image you are giving considerable benefit to the owner of the office building. Then, too, you are providing a visible benefit to the office-furniture-leasing company. Here again you have strengthened your personal relationship with these two entities.

Another plus factor is the impact upon your bank manager and other banks in the area. You may be sure that they are keenly aware of your rising star.

All this is, however, only the beginning of your P.R. campaign. If you did nothing further you could expect to sink back into obscurity in a very short time.

Now how do you keep a campaign rolling when there is nothing to report? That's simple, you engage in an activity known as 'making' news. There's nothing new about this technique, it's been going on since the days of Alexander the Great. You make news by creating an incident or an event. P.T. Barnum was superb in this department. He would always manage to have something 'discovered' by some third party and then, in the midst of the excitement and attendant publicity would 'buy' it and exhibit it in one of his 'scientific shows'.

You, of course, cannot engage in creating any kind of an event just for the sake of publicity. It must be the 'right kind' of publicity. It has to be the kind that will add stature to the public image you are creating. It should be something that should be, in some way, in the public interest as well as be interesting in itself.

It should serve some useful purpose and, if possible, be noteworthy and deserving of praise for the part you play in producing this event. It must, somehow, take place in or around your office building.

Let's see if we can't tie all that together in a worthwhile event that will have far reaching effect prior to—during—and after the event takes place.

Let's presume that your office building has a fair sized lobby. This could serve as the arena for the event. Obviously, any attendant publicity would have to mention that it was taking place in the XYZ Office Building.

How about a series of 'one man (or woman) art shows'? A 'one man show' for an artist is almost the equivalent of an Academy Award for an actor.

You would write a letter to the owners of all the art galleries within a 100 mile radius of your building and tell them of your plan to hold a series of 'one man shows' in the lobby of your office building. You would ask them to submit the names of serious young artists who were, in their opinion, deserving of such an honor.

You would further explain that a series of art competitions would take place. Judging this competition would be a panel comprised of six qualified art gallery owners and six patrons of the arts (men or women).

The panel of judges would select the three most deserving artists to be honored with individual 'one man shows'. You would appreciate suggestions from the art gallery owners as to the names of art gallery owners and patrons of the arts they believe qualified to act as judges. A self-addressed envelope would be enclosed.

When the responses were received, you would be able to judge how much enthusiasm there was for the project. You would also have a list of prominent men and women that could be contacted and notified of their nomination as judges. Would they be willing to serve?

Now unless the list of prominent people is too large, you could satisfy all of the men and women who said they would serve by dividing them into individual panels who would be invited to judge the competitors works on different days. You see, too large a panel would, at one sitting, have difficulty in arriving at a decision. Six gallery owners and six patrons makes a decent sized jury.

Now once you have the names set—you send out a series of press releases. They are: (one each day)

1. The intention of holding the competition and the purpose of the competition.
2. The names of the nominated artists with some background on each artist—facts about the event.
3. The names of the selected judges—some background on each judge—facts about the competition.
4. Results of the competition—naming the date for the first 'one man show'.
5. The first show—press invitations—first day premiere with special guests (including judges), public excluded. They will be invited the following day.
6. Second show—press—special guests.
7. Third show—press—special guests.

Naturally, as the host, you will be present at each of these opening events. You will have an opportunity to meet and greet the socially elite. This will, of course, include the owners of the luxury car agencies (whom you have personally invited).

Your guest list of prominent people who will attend this 'black tie' event, will be invaluable to you when you start to recruit stockholders in your special Sub S leasing corporation. This plus your personal contact with the luxury car agency owners should make it quite simple for you to put your car-leasing corporation plan into operation at an early date.

Now what you have done, at little or no cost, is to keep your P.R. campaign rolling and added more depth and dimension to your public image. You are now, in addition to being known as a rising chief executive, also a civic minded, culturally oriented 'person' with the ability to 'make things happen'—and that's a highly valuable trait in any person.

It's exactly the kind of person that fund-raising organizations seek as honorary chairmen (or women) to head up annual or semi-annual drives and campaigns.

You may be certain that you will receive several invitations from different organizations. These are golden opportunities for receiving the 'right' kind of publicity. However, you cannot accept all of them. It would be virtually impossible to do a decent job on any of them if you did.

Thank each organization for the invitation and then say that you would like time to consider it. Your task is to sift through them and select the most prestigious one and accept that. Send a personal letter to all the other organizations, thanking them, and explaining that you were accepting the X invitation but that you would be most happy if they would consider you for the next campaign.

Now, when you have accepted the chairmanship—really work at it. Do the best job you can with it. Make many personal contacts. Be prepared to speak at luncheons, at service clubs like Rotary, Lions, Kiwanis, etc.

Remember that you have both a winning and a power personality. Use both and you will enhance your public image tremendously. Above all, an excellent record in voluntary public service work is one of the best credentials you can have. You may be certain that your star will rise sharply.

In all the time that you have been mingling with the 'elite' you will have gained a great deal of insight into their feelings about certain 'issues' that beset any community large or small. This is because you are a really attentive 'listener' (remember?)

Somewhere along the line you are going to find a real 'key' issue that has generated an almost unanimous feeling within the community leadership.

Dig into this issue. Learn all you can about the 'pros' and 'cons'. Try, if you can, to become really knowledgeable about this issue.

Above all, examine the political situation with regard to this issue. Will it become part of the next election campaign? What does the community in general think of this issue? (Here's how to find out:)

Take a sheet of plain white bond and type:

AD HOC COMMITTEE
(Write This Issue Here)

A PUBLIC OPINION POLL

Yes   No   D.K.   M   F   REMARKS

Then rule vertical lines separating each item. Incidentally—
ad hoc' means for this (purpose) and D.K. means don't know.

Now take your master sheet to the local library or stationery
store that offers a Xerox copier. It's usually 15¢ a copy (or 3 for
a quarter). Run off about 5 or 6 copies. You won't need more.

Attach your papers to a clipboard and station yourself
about twenty feet from a busy, downtown street corner on a
pleasant day. You are now ready to conduct your public
opinion poll. Just smile as a person approaches you and say,
"Good morning. We're taking a public opinion poll. Are you in
favor of (name the issue)?"

If the person says 'yes' or 'no' and keeps walking just note the
answer and try the next person. If that person stops to answer.
Write the yes or no and then ask,

"Why?"

Listen carefully to the answer. Then, when they have
finished, nod and say, "If I understand you correctly the reason
you are for (or against) this issue is because:

(enumerate briefly the main points of their argument)

If they agree, then jot down those points, thank them and
move to the next person. Continue doing this until you have
listed at least 100 responses. That's a fair sampling and should
give you decent percentage figures.

If anyone should ask you (and they will!) just tell them the
name of your ad hoc committee. If they ask your name, give it
to them. If they ask what the poll is for, tell them it's the
forerunner of a radio and newspaper poll.

When you have finished taking your public opinion poll, go
back to your office and figure your percentages. It's quite easy.
Let's suppose there is a final count of Yes-67—No-24 and
Don't Know-9, you now have a percentage total (based on 100
responses) of Yes 67%, No 24% and Don't Know 9%.

You should also have some rich material in the remark
section. People can give you some surprisingly throughtful
answers when you ask them 'why?'

You aren't finished yet. You now call at least six men and
women who have expressed a really strong opinion on this
particular issue and invite them to meet with you, at your office
for the purpose of joining the ad hoc committee for action on
this issue. Assure them that the meeting will not take more than

one hour, that there will be an agenda and ask that they bring any facts and figures relative to the issue, with them.

When that's settled, call in your resident attorney and ask his help in drafting a legal petition which you intend to present to the Mayor, or the chief executive of the municipality you live in.

Have these petitions printed and ready prior to your first meeting of the ad hoc committee. Be sure to have fresh coffee on hand as well as means of making tea for those who don't drink coffee.

Ask your legal associate to sit in on the meeting. It will be beneficial for him to meet these people and it will enhance your status to have him there.

You should—if you've picked the right suite of offices—have a conference room. That's where you'll hold the meeting. Have your secretary there, to take notes of the meeting. If you haven't got one, then hire a Tempo or a Kelly Girl for the evening. It's only for a couple of hours and won't cost much, but it adds to your image to have one present for the meeting.

Have a pad and pencil at each place plus a typed agenda and a summary of the public opinion poll which shows percentages and a breakdown of the pertinent 'remarks'. Also have sets of the printed petition next to you, at your place.

When your committee members arrive, the majority will be prompt—one or two may lag—but don't wait more than ten minutes before starting the meeting if they don't show up immediately.

Follow the agenda closely. It should be simple and straightforward. As example:

Opening remarks
Items:
1. Public Opinion Poll
2. Petition Committees
3. Action Committees
   Letters, Postcards, etc.
4. Date of next meeting

Open the meeting by explaining that you have, for some time, been deeply concerned about the issue.

That, after spending some time in a personal investigation of the various aspects of the issue you went a step further and took a sampling of public opinion on the issue. The results are in front of them. It would seem that a majority of the general public is in accord with the feelings of the committee. You intend to carry it further by persuading the newspapers and radio stations to conduct a poll—thus gaining additional publicity for the issue. You now wanted them to act in the role of petition committee chairmen. As such they would form small committees to disseminate the petitions and obtain as many signatures as possible. Would they be agreeable to such activity? When they respond favorably—and they will—hand out the sets of printed petitions. If there are any questions—as to legality—your lawyer can answer those questions.

Allow little time for discussion—there's little need and you want to really ramrod this meeting.

Friendly but serious is the keynote.

The next item on the agenda is the question of action committees. You want them to chair these committees as well. Here you can open the floor for discussion of ways and means of taking action—beyond the obvious one of letters and postcards. Again your lawyer can help if there is a question of peaceful demonstration or other activities that might require legal interpretation.

Try to limit the discussion diplomatically. Be sure that the salient points that are made are clearly understood and that the tasks of forming the action committees are clearly defined for the chairman (and women).

Make certain, at that point, that no one has any objection to their name being mentioned in connection with publicity that will be attendant to the campaign.

Then propose a date for the next meeting that is unanimously agreeable. As for a motion for adjournment, have it seconded and close the meeting. Thank them all for coming, tell them they are welcome to stay and chat as long as they like, but that you have a meeting to attend. Tell them that copies of the minutes of the meeting will be ready for them at the next meeting and leave.

Your legal associate can take care of the Kelly Girl who will type up the minutes before she leaves. You must leave because you have a 'meeting' and you've made your impression which should be an excellent one.

The next step, naturally, is the creation of new press releases which have considerable power since they not only deal with an important issue but concern important people in the community. You can write long releases and be assured of plenty of space. You may also be contacted by the newspapers for an interview. That goes for the radio stations as well.

As the chairman of the ad hoc committee and the spokesman you will be in an excellent position to play a modest role and dwell on the activities of your committee members— naming them individually. Also give full credit to your legal associate and the time he is devoting to the cause. Remember— you are there doing the talking—so say little about yourself— but most about your associates. You build loyalty that way because public appreciation is the golden coin for people.

Talk about the public opinion poll that your committee has taken but refuse to quote percentages because you're certain that the newspapers and radio stations will want to take their own polls. Which is one way to insure that they do.

When you're discussing the issues with the radio interviewer (or newspaper interviewer) never say 'I think'—always say 'our committee thinks or feels that such and such is the case'.

Be courteous, pleasant and relaxed with your interviewer because the impression you make will be reflected in the broadcast or the newspaper story.

This, too, is part of your public relations effort.

In your second meeting with your committee you will have the following items at each place:

1. A copy of the minutes of the last meeting
2. A copy of the press release
3. Copies of tear sheets from any printed stories
4. A summary of the radio interview
5. An agenda for the current meeting which shows:
   A. Brief report on the publicity activities
   B. Report from committee chairmen on the petition activities
   C. Speaking engagement list to be provided by committee chairmen
   D. Endorsements from various clubs and groups

Under item C. you will inform your committee chairmen that you intend to speak at as many different service clubs, luncheons, etc. as can be arranged by your committee people. Your intention is to give a 15 minute talk followed by a 5 to 10 minute question and answer session. You also intend to take petitions with you and at the end of the session try to sign up as many people as possible. You would like one of your people to volunteer as the head of the committee's Speaker's Bureau which would set up all the speaking engagements.

You would also like some back-up speakers in case any conflicting engagements should occur—and in the event that the number of engagements became too much for you to carry.

After the discussion relative to this item you would move to the next item (D) which concerned the question of obtaining endorsements for the issue by various clubs and organizations. While this could be obtained in conjunction with the speaking engagements there was also the necessity of contacting groups and organizations which might not have a program provision which gave an opportunity to speakers. All committee people would make an effort to obtain these endorsements.

There would be open discussion as to ways and means.

A date would be set for the next meeting and you would ask for an adjournment. This time you would stay with them and socialize if that's what the majority appeared to want.

If you have timed your campaign correctly, it should be reaching a peak just prior to the election campaigns. Look over the field of candidates and select a fresh entry that is backed by the right political party (that's the dominant one in your area that is also the preferred party of the majority of your prominent people).

Arrange to meet with this candidate and his party backers— the professional politicians. Tell him (and them) that if the candidate will make your issue a part of his platform and promise to support it, you will guarantee to deliver several thousand votes.

This is known as political 'clout' and the man who has it is a man to be reckoned with in political circles. You may be sure that they have heard about you and you may also be sure that they will be delighted at your offer.

When this candidate makes his public announcement that he is strongly in favor of the issue and has therefore made it one of the planks in his program, you then call a meeting of your committee people and make the suggestion that you turn over the petitions to this candidate and permit him to make the presentation to the Mayor.

Now this is a calculated move on your part. It does a number of very interesting things for you. It reinforces the image you have created of a man who is willing to let others take credit. That you are not hungry for personal publicity and that you are more interested in seeing that the issue is resolved than you are in gaining a reward.

You will also please the political powers for your generosity in giving the candidate the opportunity to grab the headlines and that act will not be forgotten.

It won't be long before you will be approached and offered a candidacy. Think it over carefully before you decide. If there is no better than even chance—decline it. You cannot afford to lose the first time out. You're a winner—all the way—remember?

In any event—you will have firmly established yourself with this relatively simple public relations campaign and can, if you wish—continue to use it and eventually gain political power—if that's what you want.

In our next chapter we shall take up the question of the fundamental principles of success.

CHAPTER EIGHT

THE FUNDAMENTAL PRINCIPLES OF SUCCESS

It's surprising how children can sometimes, with a perfectly innocent question, provoke serious thought about an aspect of your life that you may have overlooked.

One afternoon, while I was editing one of the chapters in this book, my little boy, Bobby, came into the study and announced,

"I'm never going to speak to Jimmy again."

"Oh? I thought he was your best friend."

"Not any more." He scowled at the rug, scuffed it with his toe, emitted several dramatic sighs that indicated that it was up to me to keep the conversation rolling. I asked the obvious question.

"What did he do to you, Bobby?"

"He called me a liar. I said you had more money than anybody, that you were a zillionaire. He said there was no such thing as a zillionaire and I was a liar. You are a zillionaire, aren't you, Daddy?"

"No, Bobby, I'm a millionaire."

"Is that as good as a zillionaire?"

"Let's put it this way, Bobby—a 'zillionaire' is imaginary while a millionaire is real."

"You're a real millionaire?"

"Yes I am."

Bobby thought about that for a bit and then looked at me and asked, "How did you get to be a millionaire?"

How indeed? I don't remember exactly what I told him, but it satisfied him and he went off to find Jimmy to explain the difference between a zillionaire and a real millionaire, leaving me with a highly provocative question in my mind.

What were the principles that set millionaires apart from other people? Isn't that really the question that Willy Loman asked Ben's ghost?

The more I thought about it, the more I realized that this book would be incomplete if I neglected to give some direct answers to that question.

After a lot of straight thinking I arrived at the following, fundamental principles of success that apply directly to the question Bobby asked.

CONTROL

A millionaire controls his environment completely. He exercises direct control on everyone and everything that surrounds him. If, for example, he decides to publish a book he will control everyone connected with it. He will personally choose and control the editors, the secretaries who will type the manuscript, the artist who creates the layouts, the photographer who takes the pictures and the people who print it.

He is aware, and in control, of every stage of the project from its inception to the final published product. That single aspect—control—is the keystone in the arch of every successful enterprise. It is the millionaire's prerogative that sets him apart from other men.

An equally important variant of control is choice. A millionaire chooses to employ the services of a particular bank. In fact he exercises his choice in every aspect of his business and personal life. He personally chooses his middle and upper management people as well as every employee in his business. He exercises his personal choice in the matter of business associates, suppliers, service vendors and maintenance firms.

A millionaire is always a hero—not a victim of circumstances. He is an active force rather than a passive participant in life. It is his personal choice which dictates every aspect of the environment in which he works and lives. He controls, through personal choice, the quality of the air he breathes, the temperature of the room, the sound or lack of sound in the background as well as the humidity.

In short, every single detail of a millionaire's life is controlled through personal choice.

PERSISTENCE

A millionaire is keenly aware that, with the exception of control, the most significant factor in his success is persistence. He is always cognizant of the fact that a very thin line separates success from failure. He knows that the history of business is filled with stories of men who, in essence, stopped drilling three feet before hitting oil, or came within inches of striking the 'mother lode' before abandoning the ultimately rich gold mine.

You might say that persistence is the art of devoting relentless, continuous effort until you have successfully completed the planned project. It has been said that the world makes way for a man who knows exactly where he's going and will not stop until he gets there.

CYCLE COMPLETION

This is an important variant of persistence. Each morning, when I arrive at my office, I make a list of everything I intend to accomplish on that particular day. I call each project a cycle. My primary goal is to complete each cycle that I start. That's one of the things that sets a millionaire apart from other people. He completes the cycles that he starts. He will not allow anything or anyone to divert him from his goal of completion.

Most people start things but never finish them. They allow people and circumstances to interfere with the completion of the cycle; sometimes to the point of making them forget that they even started the cycle.

Millionaire's also have the ability to assign the correct priorities to cycles. They do not allow cycles of secondary important to take precedence over cycles of prime importance.

PERSONAL RADAR

A unique ability to anticipate future developments is an inherent quality of every successful person. It is the kind of ability that distinguishes a master chess player from a novice. The master is able to 'see' five or six moves ahead and accurately calculate the possible responses to any move he makes. The novice cannot.

A millionaire must be keenly aware of the possible consequences of each move he makes. He anticipates and prepares for the future today. It is this 'personal radar' which enables him to succeed where the novice will fail.

If you want to succeed, begin to develop your own personal radar. Be fully aware that each move you make will have an effect on your future. Anticipate the future by preparing for it today.

Start thinking about the future of your business venture now. Will you expand to larger quarters? Take on a partner? Employ more assistants?

What about your future plans for yourself? Will you move into other fields? Enter politics? Write a book? Acquire new companies and form a conglomerate?

If you really want to be a millionaire you must make things happen for you rather than wait and let things happen to you.

TIME MANAGEMENT

One of the main reasons why some people succeed and others don't is time. Successful people use time rather than allowing time to use them. They are keenly aware that there are exactly 1,440 minutes in each 24 hour day. They make each minute count by refusing to allow trivia or non-essential projects to interfere with important cycle completion. This permits them to move from initiation to completion of each cycle in a relaxed and unhurried fashion.

Rather than attempting to cover this subject in depth (which would require a book in itself) let me give you a simple concept that helped me in the beginning.

I call it the 'Taxi Meter' concept. Get yourself a small digital clock, place it on your desk and pretend that it's a taxi meter. Assume that each minute costs $1.00.

If you can instill that concept in your mind, and in the mind of your associates, you will begin to eliminate the wasteful, time-consuming chitchat; the rambling oral reports; the unnecessary visits of employees with problems that they should have solved themselves; the unanswered intercoms and the thousand and one time-consuming inconsequentials which may pass unnoticed until they become visible money wasters through the taxi-meter concept.

Time is money. Big money. Stop wasting it.

SPECIALIZED KNOWLEDGE

This is the Age of the Specialist. The days of the general practitioner in medicine, in law, and in virtually every field of endeavor, is gone forever. The original pool of knowledge which could easily be assimilated with several years of intensive effort, has now grown to the size of an ocean that is fed daily by never-ending streams and rivers of data. No one, in a single lifetime could hope to digest that knowledge. Thus—specialization.

You will succeed in the exact ratio of your ability to assimilate specialized knowledge. Whatever profession you choose as your second career—study it. Learn as much as you can about it. Read the trade journals. You can find out the names of the trade journals in your particular profession by visiting your library. Ask the research librarian for a copy of Stadard Rate & Data's Business Publications. This lists every trade journal that is published in the world.

If you have a chance to attend seminars relative to your profession, please do so. They will offer you an opportunity to learn and, at the same time, to meet many knowledgeable practitioners who will, if you approach them correctly, give you much valuable free advice.

The more you learn about your profession, the more valuable you become and the greater your chances for success and eventually, for becoming a millionaire.

THE BRAIN TRUST

Napoleon Hill believed that one of the major keys to success is directly related to your ability to surround yourself with bright, ambitious people who share common goals with you. However you must offer these people more than just the opportunity to work with you. You must offer them something of value—not necessarily money.

When you acquire your resident attorney and tax specialist don't expect that the rent-free office will be all that they require from you. You must discover their particular goals and demonstrate that you are interested in helping them to achieve those goals. There must be mutual benefit if the relationship is to survive.

If you surround yourself with bright, hard-working people with demonstrable talents, you will benefit from those unique abilities if you help them to grow and develop their talents; if you help them to reap the rewards they're entitled to. You must give as much as you receive. Then you, as well as they, will ultimately succeed.

PROBLEM CONFRONTATION

The laws of survival have programmed Man to avoid pain and seek pleasure. That's a natural law that should, and must be, tempered with logic if you are to succeed in any profession.

People who avoid the pain of problem confrontation will fail. That's axiomatic. You cannot avoid the pain of facing the truth regardless of how distasteful the situation may be. No problem will go away simply because you choose to ignore it. On the contrary it will probably grow even larger.

Think for a moment. How many problems are you ignoring right now? You aren't going to solve them by pretending they don't exist. They do. They eat at your subconscious, they rob you of the pleasure you should have. Confront them—erase them through solution.

There is a saying in the retail trade that your first loss is your best loss (in relation to unsaleable merchandise). Apply that to all your ventures. If the stock you bought at 10 has dropped to 5 and you know instinctively that the company is not going to really make it—sell now at 5 and take the loss, rather than wait for a total write-off.

Problems can only be erased through confrontation.

DECISION MAKING BY ALTERNATIVES

When you have to make a decision you will find that there are only two types of options available to you. Viable options that already exist or options that can be created. There are very few 'ideal' solutions when we deal with reality. Ideal solutions are usually found in works of fiction.

Indecisive people are those who wait patiently for that 'ideal' solution to present itself. It never will. Yet these people, in the face of logic, still wait hopefully.

I am reminded of a friend, a business associate, who is looking for a special type of assistant. In addition to being intelligent and possessed of unique talent, this assistant must be willing to put in long, hard hours.

My friend's complaint is that he has found several men who fit these qualifications but they want too much money! The ones who will work for the kind of money he's offering don't have the talents.

So my friend is waiting patiently for the fictional assistant to arrive complete with all the qualifications and willing to work for peanuts.

It simply will not happen.

To succeed at anything you must choose from reasonable options that exist. You cannot create unreasonable options and expect them to be viable. Ideally you might but since that is obviously not a viable option you could turn to an alternative option and decide to settle down and earn ten million dollars.

Most successful executives make more than 100 decisions a day after analyzing the possible alternatives. The more successful an executive is, the higher the percentage of right decisions; but even the best executives make 10 to 20 mistakes a day. However they do make decisions, rightly or wrongly, the decisions are made.

Benjamin Franklin's method of making a decision was to list all the alternatives on a big sheet of paper and then spend an entire day trying to think of any other alternatives. At the end of that time he would pick the best option on that big piece of paper and make his decision.

Try it, next time—it may help. Just decide.

ETHICS

There is little doubt, at this point, that the powerful mental conditioning exerted by TV, the movies and popular fiction, has created a picture in people's minds of a really savage business world; a world of dog-eat-dog, back biting and apple polishing; a world filled with wheeler-dealers and helpless innocent victims.

While it is true that there are some millionaires and some top executives who operate their businesses with all the friendliness and honesty of a half-starved timber wolf; the majority of men and women I deal with on a daily basis are largely people of integrity, honesty and compassion. They are people with whom I am proud to be associated with.

They are, above all, intelligent and aware that people who take everything and give nothing in return generally wind up with nothing in the end.

I can tell you, of my own knowledge, that when you deal fairly and honestly with people; when you are sincerely interested in them and considerate of their feelings, your reward is far greater than you ever realize.

The rewards (which you sometimes never know about) can be an accountant who works at home until 2:00 AM to solve a tax problem; a secretary who decides, on her own to stay until 8:00 at night to finish an important contract so that it will be waiting for you when you arrive at the airport the following morning; an assistant who cuts short a well deserved vacation and flies 3,000 miles to help you when he hears that his backup has been taken ill.

You cannot obtain that kind of loyalty and devotion with money alone. Every intelligent executive knows that talent comes high and rare talent comes even higher—but money alone isn't the answer. It's the way you treat people that counts in the end. If you're straight, honest and decent with them they will respond to that treatment in kind. But it has to be real—it cannot be faked because people recognize that kind of dishonesty instinctively.

The sooner you recognize that fact and learn to put it into practice the sooner you will become the success you are striving towards. It took me several years and a lot of unhappiness before I realized exactly what was wrong with my life. When I faced it, and made my decision to change, I achieved more happiness and more success than I ever dreamt of previously.

You will, too, if you decide right now that you will conduct your personal and business life with honesty, integrity and compassion. You'll find, in the end, that all of them really are the best policy.

In the next chapter I'm going to tell you the secret of how to acquire a winning personality.

CHAPTER NINE

HOW TO
ACQUIRE
A WINNING
PERSONALITY

This chapter alone can change your life dramatically. What you are about to learn can—if properly employed—make you happier than you have ever been in your life. It will help you to develop a winning personality almost instantly. It will provide you with a lifetime of enjoyment in your business, your home and your social life.

You will begin to look forward to attending business meetings, parties and any other social event which you may have previously disliked or dreaded.

The reason for this change will become clear and obvious to you once you see and understand the secret of making people like you the moment that they meet you.

To understand exactly how it works, let's examine a typical situation that is very familiar to you. It's called:

Meeting strangers in unfamiliar surroundings.

Mention that all-embracing situation to a group of a hundred people and it's safe to say that almost 99% of them will immediately experience a slight panic at the idea.

If you also react in this manner then it should be of some comfort to know that you are not alone. It's a normal reaction that you share with most of the people on Earth.

People who have studied this almost universal dislike of meeting strangers in unfamiliar surroundings have traced the origin to an atavism—which means a trait that has been with Mankind almost from the very beginning. Any stranger to the village or tribe was bad and looked upon with intense dislike tinged with fear.

This dislike with fear usually surfaces as a child when we attend our first day of kindergarten or grade school. It's an attitude that most people carry with them throughout their lifetime. When someone says, "I don't like parties or social gatherings"—what they are really expressing is the fear that no one will like them.

If they were completely honest they would say,

"I just know I'll be miserable because I don't know what to say to strange people. I'm no good with 'small talk'."

If this is your problem; if you want people to like you but you only seem to succeed in 'turning people off' whenever you try to talk to them—then relax because you are about to discover exactly how to 'turn people on' almost instantly, the first time you meet them and that secret is worth ten times what you paid for this book!

Let's start with a basic fact: You are not the only one that wants to be liked and admired. Everyone you meet has the exact same desire.

It's a universal desire. Anyone who doesn't want to be liked and admired is either kidding himself or he's a sick personality.

Another thing that's fairly universal is the fact that most people fail in their efforts to make people like and admire them.

The reason that they fail is that they are trying to make people like and admire them. They are trying so hard that they completely forget that the person they're trying to impress is only interested in one person in the entire room—that's himself. The man or woman you're talking to is not really interested in you. Even if there was some slight interest at the beginning, it evaporates as you go on talking about you.

If, instead of talking, you were listening attentively to what they were saying, then you would be on your way to gaining their respect and admiration for you. The very fact that you are listening to them attentively denotes respect for their opinion, their ideas. It's the greatest compliment you can pay to any person you meet. It's the kind of compliment they appreciate.

So the first rule is to listen attentively to the person you want to be liked and admired by.

You may say to yourself, at this point, "That's fine. I can do that. But how do I get people to talk to me in the first place? How do I 'break the ice' in the beginning?

That's so simple it's almost laughable.

Just pick your target—a man or woman that you would like to become friendly with. Just walk up to them with a friendly smile (not a silly grin) stick out your hand and say, "How do you do. I'm John (Jane) Doe."

Have no fear of rebuff. The majority of people are grateful to you for taking the initiative. They will almost always smile back, take your hand and tell you who they are.

Now I can see you nodding your head and saying, "All right. I can do that, too. But what do I do next?"

This is the area where most people flounder. It's where the cardinal sin occurs—the sin of talking about yourself. The sin of trying to impress people with your intelligence, your skills or talents; with your many fine accomplishments. You must not do that—ever.

What you must do is say something agreeable, in a simple and friendly manner. Something that anyone will find it easy to agree with. This is the beginning of the very important 'small talk' that acts as a social lubricant and makes it easy for people to relate to each other in an easy and agreeable manner.

'Small talk' is only used to break the ice. It is not designed to be used throughout the relationship. This can be as deadly as talking about yourself. Small talk is mainly used to enter a conversation. The simplest and safest subject to use is the weather. It's a subject that is always familiar to everyone and— most importantly—it's one that you can use for an automatic agreement.

Try, always, to use a positive approach—a happy approach—because people warm swiftly to happy people. Let's imagine a conversation between you and your target person (we'll use T.P. to make it easy).

You: Isn't it a beautiful day?

T.P.: Oh yes. Lovely.

Now your target person might take off, at that point, and begin talking at length about the weather—and might relate an interesting anecdote about the weather—and you simply have to listen attentively—ask an occasional intelligent question (to demonstrate that you are listening) and you're on your way. You merely have to guide the conversation gently to questions about where your T.P. comes from—what your T.P. does and you will open the flood gates because people enjoy talking about themselves to someone who listens attentively.

The more attentively you listen, the more your T.P. will become convinced you are an extremely intelligent person because you obviously find that they are intelligent.

Your T.P. will also consider that you are an extremely interesting person because you find that they are interesting. You must believe me when I tell you that it works that way.

Now a strange thing will happen when you make a sincere effort to become interested in what your T.P. is saying to you. You will discover that your T.P. really is interesting and you are learning a great deal from listening. Your admiration for your T.P. will begin to increase and as it does—your T.P. will become aware of it.

In turn, your T.P. will begin to admire you because of your obvious admiration.

Now, in gratitude and interest, your T.P. will try to turn the conversation over to you. Accept this gambit gracefully and briefly. Just a few sentences about yourself and then turn the conversation back to your T.P. with a sincere, "I really would like to know more about" (whatever subject your T.P. was talking about).

Your T.P. will take the reins of conversation with gratitude—more convinced than ever that you are really a charming, intelligent and interesting person.

Just look at what you have accomplished with just a few judicious questions in the space of a few minutes!

Your target person now thinks you are a charming, intelligent, interesting and admirable person. Beyond that, your T.P. is convinced that you are a marvellous conversationalist—even though you barely said anything!

Yet—in a strange way—your T.P. is absolutely right because you are one of the rarest creatures on Earth—you are an intelligent, attentive listener.

Do you have any idea of how hungry people are for that kind of attention? Some people will spend thousands of dollars for the services of a psychiatrist or a psychotherapist just to have an intelligent, attentive listener—but that's not entirely satisfactory because those professional LISTENERS are being paid to listen. You are not.

One of the ways that you can develop the warmth and sincerity of a genuine attentive listener is to practice both smiling and listening in the mirror. Pretend that your mirror image is a T.P. that you are listening to. Notice the effect when you look directly at your mirror image's eyes. This is an important point. Try to maintain a warm and pleasant expression. You can attain this, quite easily by thinking warm and pleasant thoughts.

Now, after you have become familiar with the way to create a warm and pleasant expression in the mirror—start to practice the art of attentive listening with your own family.

You can practice (without letting them know what you are doing) with your children—your wife—your parents—with the postman—any visitor to your home. The end result will astonish you. You will notice how much more enjoyable your home life is. You will notice that your children and your wife will 'light up' whenever you come home. The affection and admiration you will receive from both your children and your wife will be a real eye-opener. No matter how good your relationship is now—it will improve a hundredfold when you begin to practice the art of attentive listening.

There is another benefit. The more you practice the easier it will become and—eventually—it will be as natural as breathing. You will also find—as you become more adept—that almost everyone can be truly interesting if you give them a chance to be.

Now you have one of the major 'keys' to the secret of how to make people like and admire you instantly the first time you meet.

We have discussed this 'key' from the standpoint of you going directly to a target person and making the first contact. Now we're going to discuss the 'secret' of drawing people to you—as if you were a magnet.

What is it that makes people 'attractive'? Oddly enough, the most attractive people are neither handsome or beautiful on close inspection. They only seem to be because of other attributes. The most attractive people are relaxed, warm, friendly and—above all—cheerful.

There's a cheerful, optomistic aura about them.

If you want to understand how this is achieved, we will have to go back to the mirror. Now stand in front of it—examining yourself objectively. Just watch your face carefully. We are going to begin by projecting unpleasant thoughts. Think about one thing that is really unpleasant—even repugnant to you. Keep your eyes closed while you think about it. Now, in the middle of thinking those really unpleasant thoughts—open your eyes quickly and capture the expression on your face. You'll be astonished at the negative aspect on your face.

Now close your eyes and think about the really pleasant things in your life. Think happy thoughts. Now open your eyes and you will be shocked to find that you are looking at an almost entirely different person.

Thinking does show up on your face almost like an exposed image appears on paper once it's been placed in the developer.

Abraham Lincoln once refused to consider a certain man for an important cabinet post. When asked why, Lincoln said, "I don't like his looks." When someone objected and said, "That's not fair—he can't help how he looks."—Lincoln said, "Oh yes he can. Anyone over forty is responsible for how he looks."

What is most interesting here is that Lincoln was considered ugly by people who didn't know him—people who had only seen caricatures or ugly pictures of him. People who came to know him, thought him quite handsome. Artists who portrayed him, in later years, gave him a noble face because there was nobility in Lincoln.

So remember that you will become what you think. If you want to reflect a pleasant, cheerful, intelligent aura then you had better start right now to think pleasant, cheerful intelligent thoughts. Oddly enough, you will find that it's a much easier way to live and far more enjoyable to yourself and to the people around you.

As you practice this new way of thinking, certain changes will take place. You will begin to feel better and as you do, your outward appearance will change. People will begin to notice you because you will stand out in almost any group of people.

If you took a survey of public opinion right now, it is safe to say that the majority of people who were asked what it was they wanted most would say, "To be happy."

That desire to be happy makes them want to be with people who appear to be happy. They are drawn to cheerful people almost without realizing it.

Now let's suppose that someone is drawn to you—and you're aware of it. You may also be aware that the person is shy about beginning the conversation. You do exactly what you did when you decided on your target person. You smile, put out your hand and say, "How do you do, I'm John (Jane) Doe.

You use your opening line about the weather but this time you realize that there is going to be no flow of words in response. The person is really shy. Now it's up to you to lead them into conversation gently.

For example: if after your opening remark about the weather being beautiful you only received a simple,

"Yes. Isn't it." and nothing more, then you use the information gathering question such as . . .

"Is the weather always this nice or is this unusual?"

Now there are several responses—all of them easy—that you can expect. If your reluctant conversationalist says, "I don't know. I haven't lived here very long."

That gives you an opportunity to ask the person questions like, "Where did you live before? What was it like? Do you miss it?" and so forth.

Most people feel comfortable when they talk about their home town. They're fully familiar with it and you are not, so they have no fear that they'll make a mistake. They will usually (if assisted gently) go on at some length about what their home town was like.

You can then lead them easily into telling you about themselves. The things they like to do—the special skills they might have—their ambitions—everything. Once people get over their initial shyness and realize that you are interested in what they're saying—it's almost like opening long-closed flood gates. They're happy to talk and extremely grateful for the opportunity you've them. They're even more delighted when you pay close attention and appear to be keenly interested.

They also become aware of how comfortable they are with you and they begin to place great trust in you. This is critically important in your new role as a top executive. Trust is one of the most valuable assets you can gain as you develop your new successful role in life.

A word of caution. You must make every effort to deserve the trust you are given. You must guard against betraying confidences you may be given. Never gossip. Never pass comments that are unfavorable about anyone.

If you should be asked an opinion about someone and cannot make a favorable comment just say that you don't know them well enough to pass judgment on them. No one can fault you for that kind of discretion.

This brings us to the matter of compliments. Sincere compliments (not flattery) are as welcome to men as they are to women. Anyone can appreciate a sincere compliment. However if you do compliment someone try to find some trait, feature or talent that very few people are aware of. If a woman is obviously beautiful or has beautiful hair or eyes that are unusually beautiful she doesn't appreciate compliments about them because they are so obvious. She would be more appreciative if you discovered something unusual about her that very few people are aware of. Something that she knows but few people know. This requires that you study her with a great deal of care. If you do, she will give you subtle indications of what it is she really wants to be complimented for. Discover what it is—compliment her on it—and you have made a real friend. That goes for men, too.

When you study people you have to listen very carefully not only to what they say but how they say it. Try to discover what it is that motivates them. What is it they want—what are they afraid of—try to place yourself in their shoes—their mind.

Every person you meet is unique—entirely different than any other person on Earth. You will never be bored when you begin to study people carefully. You will find them to be really fascinating—particularly as they begin to be comfortable with you and reveal their uniqueness.

This close attention, incidentally, will be one of the sincerest compliments you can pay to any person. Your obvious interest and keen attention will not only delight them, it will convince them that you are the most interesting and most charming person they have ever met.

Another extremely important 'key' to acquiring a winning personality is punctuality. You must make a special effort to be 'on time' for every appointment you make. When you are prompt it tells the person that you are meeting that you think they are important.

If you are late it tells them that you think they are not important and you build a bank of resentment which is the last thing you want to do.

If you cannot avoid being late, through some emergency, then call immediately and explain the situation. Call as soon as you realize the situation. Do not wait till after the fact—call before your appointment time.

Just as promptness is a necessary and important part of the image you are creating—so is courtesy to men and women. Courtesy is another way of expressing the fact that you think the other person is important.

Make it a habit to rise to your feet immediately whether it's a man or a woman you have not met and are about to be introduced to. Do not wait for a woman to extend her hand—extend yours immediately. There is nothing more potent than a warm, firm handclasp. It is appreciated by men and women.

Learn to cultivate a gentle, warm smile that will give a pleasant cast to your features. This is most important when you are listening to someone. It means that you like them and are sympathetic towards them. A frowning face or a heavy face frightens people and makes them uneasy. You want people to be at ease with you—to be comfortable with you.

They will be, if you are relaxed and comfortable with them. To sum up then:

(1) Look forward to meeting new people.
(2) Take it for granted that they will like you.
(3) Put them at ease by being at ease yourself.
(4) Remember to be pleasant and cheerful.
(5) Encourage others to talk about themselves.
(6) Pay close attention to what they are saying.
(7) Try to compliment their 'rare' qualities.
(8) Respect every confidence you receive.
(9) Always keep your promises.
(10) Never gossip or comment adversely.
(11) Be honest: admit that you don't know.
(12) Be courteous to men and women.
(13) Be 'on time' for all appointments.

Not one of those thirteen points is difficult to remember or to do. If you can remember them, and practice each of them wherever you are; whether it's at home, in the office, at social functions, at meetings, you will find, in a surprisingly short time, that you have acquired a rare and winning personality.

In the next chapter we're going to discuss the art of acquiring a powerful personality.

CHAPTER TEN

HOW TO ACQUIRE A POWERFUL PERSONALITY

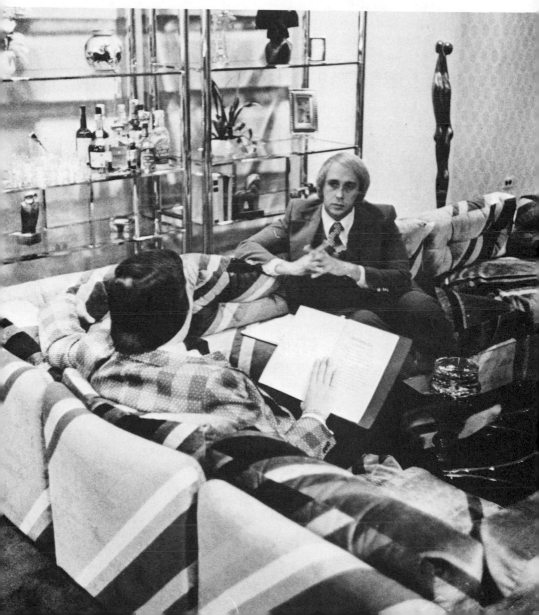

What we are going to do now is different and more complex than the material in the previous chapter. It is not more difficult to understand; it's simply that you will be moving to a higher plane of personality development.

In this chapter you are going to learn how to develop a powerful personality. The word powerful means exactly that. It means that you will be shown how to develop the kind of a personality that will make you a powerful and compelling person. You will become that kind of a person because you will be able to use your total potential.

Right now you might be compared to a car with 12 cylinders that is barely moving along with just 4 of them working. Can you imagine what it would be like to operate on all twelve cylinders?

That's exactly what you and I will accomplish before we reach the end of the next two chapters.

This chapter will deal exclusively with why you are only operating on four cylinders and how you can learn to operate on all twelve cylinders.

Let's start with some honest facts about you that you must start to admit freely to yourself.

You are not dealing honestly with yourself.

That is a completely true statement and I can prove it quite easily. If you were completely honest with yourself you would be an integrated, fully functioning personality. There would be no need for you to read this book.

All right? Then let's not play games. Accept the fact that you have been dishonest with yourself up till now—and you will take the first step towards becoming honest with yourself for the first time in your entire life.

That's exactly what it's going to take—complete honesty with yourself—and that's not an easy thing to do. However, if you make up your mind to do it—and hang in there—your ultimate reward will be greater than you can possibly imagine. You will finally release the tremendous power of your full potential and—for the first time—be able to operate on all twelve cylinders.

Then you will become a real person instead of the somewhat artificial person you are right now. Does that idea shock you? It should because right now you are not a real person. You are synthetic—just an idea of a person that you dreamed up a hell of a long time ago. An idea that you have defended and maintained against all reason, all logic.

We're going to find out how you created this artificial person and why you defend him so vigorously.

First of all, please understand that you are not the only person in this world with this problem. It's universal. Almost everyone in the world has created this kind of an artificial person. They also defend this 'idea' against reason and logic just as you do. They also fail to achieve their full potential and, instead, cling to this stunted, artificial concept and that's why they're losers instead of winners. They've handicapped themselves. They're trying to win a race by hopping on one foot instead of using both legs and running naturally.

If you'll work with me—if you will gather up your courage, and it does take guts to do what you're about to do—and accept what I'm about to tell you as the truth—then I can promise you that you will wind up with both feet squarely on the ground and a personality so powerful that it will continuously astonish you.

Let's take a look at this artificial person you have created. It's not your true self—it's a self-concept. It's a lot of little bits and pieces that you have put together over the years.

The end result is a patched up, synthetic person that you insist is really you. Yet, deep inside you there is the inescapabl knowledge that it's not you at all.

But you just can't admit that—not consciously. Whenever reality, reason or logic threatens to expose this artificial person you close your mind—blank it out—bury it—turn your back on it and refuse to admit that this threat exists. It takes a lot of energy and time to defend this self-concept—which is one of the reasons why you haven't achieved the success you should have.

How did it all start? It started when you were just beginning to realize that you and the outside world were not one continuous thing. When you began to realize that everything in the world was not an extension of your body, your mind, your wants, your needs.

That's when you began to try to figure out just who you were. That's an extremely difficult for a full grown adult to do—it's almost impossible for a small child just coming to grips with language.

You searched for clues—you listened—you watched—you absorbed everything around you in an attempt to get the answers you wanted.

Therre were plenty of clues—some right—some wrong. In your limited capacity it's no wonder that you absorbed both kinds of clues and let the wrong ones distort the right ones. Let's examine some of the clues.

No matter how well-meaning or helpful your parents tried to be, they were, in the final analysis, only human and did make mistakes. These mistakes were hurtful experiences to you. They're called traumas, which means mental wounds. No one could see them bleeding—but they bled—they hurt and they left deep scars—particularly when you were young and tender.

Let's take some classic examples of those 'mistakes'!

Older people, as well as parents, tend to forget that children hear and understand much more than is realized when they are very young. There is a tendency to talk about a child, even though the child is well within hearing distance, as though the child was unconscious.

A typical conversation between a mother and father.

"I don't know why Jimmie is so shy."

"Doesn't take after my side of the family."

"Well he certainly doesn't take after mine!"

"Maybe there's something wrong with him."

"You think we should take him to Doctor Jones?"

"Ah—he'll probably grow out of it."

"I don't know. Mary knows about a case where it turned out that the child was autistic. They had a terrible time with him. They finally had to commit him."

If you were little Jimmie, taking all that in, your immediate reaction would be shock and fear. You would be shocked to hear that 'there was something wrong with you' and fear that you would be 'sent away'.

Your survival factor would inform you that you had better rid yourself of that shyness—fast. So you bury a perfectly natural inclination and install an artificial one. You become aggressive and outgoing.

That's your first step toward the creation of the artificial person you will eventually become.

Item: You go to the beach for the first time. You may be intrigued with the water but have a natural caution about approaching it. Your father, who is a natural outdoor type, urges you to 'try it' but you hang back.

So he picks you up bodily, takes you down to the water, with you squirming, kicking and screaming, and dumps you in because that's how he learned to swim.

You thrash about frantically and somehow manage to get back to the safety of the sandy beach and your father beams and turns to your mother and says, "See? It works every time."

Your mother may have some misgivings—particularly in view of the state you're in, but 'daddy knows best' is the rule, so she doesn't say anything.

You do. You scream and howl in terror when your father tries to get you to 'try it again'—you cling to your mother and resist all efforts to dislodge you. Finally your father turns away in disgust and calls you a 'coward'.

His obvious contempt and disgust with you is another 'trauma'—another mental wound. It's also a terrible problem—because you want the love, respect and admiration of your father, but you're also terrified of going in the water.

Somehow you have to 'bury' that natural fear and replace it with artificial 'bravery' so that you can win back your father's respect. You force yourself to go back into the water even though you dread it—even though it makes you want to throw up. You even try to pretend that you actually 'enjoy' it—which is a lie.

So you have added another 'patch' to the artificial person.

Little girls don't have an easy time of it either.

You were given dolls and doll carriages because that's what little girls are supposed to like. It doesn't matter that you wanted a cap pistol and holster—or a baseball glove like your brother—'little girls don't play with those kind of toys'—and so you submerge your natural feelings and try to cultivate the artificial ones that are 'right' and win approval from daddy and mommy.

In addition to the artificial 'patches' there are the imitative patches. Jimmy wants to be a 'chip off the old block'—he wants to be 'just like daddy'—only that's not really possible because little Jimmy is not like daddy and never can be—but he's going to try to be.

And he's going to get lots of encouragement because everyone is going to think that it's 'cute'—but it's not cute—it's the most dangerous thing that can happen to little Jimmie.

Mary is going to be encouraged to be just like a little 'mommy' and she's going to give it the old college try—possibly for the rest of her life.

There are lots of other models, movie stars—famous people—storybook characters, that Jimmy and Mary will take pieces from and add to their patchwork artificial person over the years.

The end result is that Jimmy and Mary—and you put on this artificial person like a dress or a suit and you wear it, year in, year out and resist every fact—every reason—every bit of logic that tells you to discard it and emerge as yourself.

The odd part is that the real self that you have been hiding and denying all these years is a really marvelous, really intelligent, entirely unique human being.

Your real self, if you allowed it to emerge would, without doubt, dazzle the world. Most psychologists agree that the fully emerged, fully functioning being is, almost always, a true genius.

This explains why there are so few of them around. Most of the people in the world are cowering behind their artificial self-concept instead of allowing their true self to emerge and take its rightful place in the world.

Let me give you a composite picture of a fully integrated, fully functioning personality.

It would be a man or woman who was fully aware of, and able to use, their entire storehouse of talents, capabilities and potentials. Their behavior is simple and natural; there is no artificiality or straining for effort.

They are, at all times, fully aware of their own feelings and never try to suppress them. If they want to act in a certain way, they will. If not, they won't—but it is always their decision based on their feelings rather than a conformity to artificial and unreasonable rules.

They are, above all, aware of reality—the reality of themselves—and the reality of the world outside themselves.

They do not confuse words with things. They know full well that 'the map is not the territory'.

All right. Let's see if there's a way for you to overcome the damage you have done to yourself by stuffing yourself into that artificial straitjacket all these years. Let's explore a fairly simple, proven method of freeing yourself and emerging, at long last, as yourself.

170

To accomplish that, we will have to make a few changes in the way you think about things.

To understand exactly what that means and how we intend to do it, I want you to consider the following:

There is, right now, in most modern police departments, a special type of computer. It operates on the simple idea that most criminals tend to commit the same type of crimes in the same manner. That's called M.O. for modus operandi (method of operation). That usually covers the method of gaining entrance, the tools used, the methods of blowing or drilling a safe and so forth.

Whenever a crime is committed, the detectives who investigate, will attempt to piece together all of the facts in order (hopefully) of establishing an M.O.

When they arrive at the outline of this M.O. it is then fed into a computer—this is called programming a computer. Then thousands of cards or tapes are fed into the computer. The computer will, at high speed, reject all the cards or tapes that do not conform to the program it was given. Only the cards or tapes that match (or almost match) the M.O. will be selected.

The artificial person you have created can be called your particular 'programming' which means that each time you are confronted with reality, logic or reasoning which does not conform to that particular 'program', that data or idea is completely rejected.

In other words you will automatically close your mind to anything that can possibly threaten the continued existence of that artificial person you have created; that dwarfed and shabby image of yourself that you wear like a suit of armor because you believe that it 'protects' you.

The truth is that it's become your prison. It keeps you from reaching your full potential. It prevents the real 'you' from emerging and taking its rightful place in the world. It prevents the real 'you' from really functioning the way you were intended to function—at all twelve cylinders—at full power— easily and surely.

Wouldn't you rather be 'real' than artificial?

We're alone. Say it aloud. Yes! I'd rather be real! And how about admitting to yourself that you are not real right now? Say it aloud: I'm an artificial person but I'm going to change all that! I'm going to be real!

As soon as you said those words aloud, a change took place inside you. Can you feel it? Try it again.

Yes! I'd rather be real! I'm not going to be an artificial person any more! I'm going to be real!

Can you feel the stirring inside yourself? Did you get a little tingle at the back of your neck? Did you feel that shiver of anticipation? Know what that is?

That's your 'real' self stirring inside you. That's the real self that's been the 'prisoner' inside of you all these years. What you have just done is to tell your real self that 'help is on the way'— and it is.

You're going to open that prison and release your 'real' self with the aid of something called the 'alpha state'. That's simply a term for a 'state of mind' that you can produce with the aid of simple exercises we are going to discuss in a few moments.

First let's consider the levels of your brain's activity:

BETA: This is the waking state. If you consider that a normal brain produces brain waves that are quite rapid in this state because you are being bombarded with sensation from many different outside sources including light, sound, odors and—at the same time your brain is monitoring your various physical activities: walking, sitting, standing, bending, pushing, lifting, talking, etc. you can appreciate that the Beta State is fairly excitable and therefore the brain waves move at a rapid pace.

ALPHA: is the state you pass through just PRIOR to going to sleep. the relative quiet, the relaxed state of your body and the regular breathing you engage in, produces this 'slower' wave—about 7 to 14 cycles per second. after a short period of time you pass from the 'alpha state' (sometimes called the hypnoidal state) into the upper ranges of light sleep called:

THETA STATE: In this state you are most easily wakened by light, noises, or odors. After a brief time or lengthy time, depending on the environment, you enter the:

DELTA STATE: Which is the deep sleep state where your brain waves move extemely slowly—never higher than 4 cycles per second or your brain will move back into the Theta State again

Now our concern is with the Alpha State. We want to show you how to enter this state and produce Alpha Waves because when you are in this state you can 'get in touch with yourself' and can begin to re-program yourself, open that prison door and release your 'real' self.

There are many ways to achieve alpha waves. You could take an expensive course in transcendental mediation, buy or rent one of the expensive 'alpha machines' or you can simply perform some easy exercises which I will now give you. Read the following carefully, several times, until it is fixed in your mind—then perform the exercises exactly as they are described. You will begin to get results almost immediately.

1.   The first thing you must do is adopt a positive attitude towards these exercises.

Just remember that thousands of people have done it successfully with exactly the same instructions you are about to receive. You will be successful.

Fix the thought of success firmly in your mind. Say it aloud: I will be successful in entering the alpha state. Say it again. Once more. Now keep that thought in the front of your mind.

2.   Alpha waves are much slower than your normal waking brain waves (Beta waves). They operate at about half the speed of beta waves (7 to 14 cycles per second)

Why is this important?

It will help you to achieve the alpha state and let's you know why you will be so much calmer when you're in it.

3.   It is much easier to enter the alpha state when you are totally relaxed. So you will begin to relax while you are reading these instructions.

4. The opposite of relaxation is tension. To learn how to relax we first produce tension. Hold out your right arm now—while you're reading this. Now make a fist and bend your arm at the elbow as though you were demonstrating how large your biceps are. Now tense your entire arm to produce as large and hard a bicep muscle as possible. Hold it. Hold it until you feel your arm begin to tremble. Then—still applying tension—bring your arm down and rest it lightly on the arm of your chair (or table if you are reading at a table). Keep holding the tension for the count of 5. When you reach 5—let go!
As you feel the tension disappear say aloud:
THIS IS THE KIND OF RELAXATION I WANT. Feel the relief of the absence of tension. That's relaxation.

5. When you are ready to start your alpha wave exercises you will go through a similar relaxation producing session with your arms, legs, stomach muscles and your face and neck muscles...BEFORE you start your alpha wave exercises.

6. When you are ready to actually start your exercises you will need a bed, cot—or a mat and pillow on the floor. You should remove all your clothing and just wear a nightgown or loose pajamas. Remove any metal—rings, watches, ear rings, etc. Draw the blinds—pull down the shades—make it as dark as possible (if it's in the daytime). Try to insure that you will not be interrupted. Disconnect the phone or take it off the hook—lock all doors—shut the door to your bedroom—if that's where you will do your exercises.

7. Now—lie on your back and begin your relaxation exercises. Each time you tense and relax tell yourself THIS IS THE KIND OF RELAXATION I WANT. When you have finished—you should be completely relaxed and feel complete relief.

8. You should be on your back—arms slightly away from your body—relaxed—palms upward. Your legs should be slightly apart.

Now—close your eyes and try to see the number 5. Try to form it. Try writing it large in your mind. Pretend that there's a large blackboard and you have taken a big piece of white chalk and produced a large, white five.

9. Breathe slowly and deeply in a steady fashion. As soon as you see the outline of the 5—say FIVE in your mind as you exhale. Do this five times.

10. Keep breathing slowly and deeply in a steady unwavering fashion and now try to see the outline of 4 in your mind. As soon as you see the outline of the 4 say FOUR in your mind as you exhale. Say this four times.

11. Keep breathing slowly, deeply and steadily throughout the exercise. Try to form the outline of a 3 in your mind. As soon as you see the outline of the 3—say THREE in your mind. Do this three times.

12. Still breathing slowly, deeply and steadily try to see the outline of a 2 in your mind. As soon as you see it say TWO in your mind. Say this three times.

13. Now try to see the shape of a 1 in your mind. As soon as you do, say ONE three times in your mind.

14. When you have finished saying ONE in your mind just keep breathing slowly, deeply and steadily and you will be aware of an astonishing calmness. Now—in your mind—say the following: I am now in an alpha state. My mind has reached a higher dimension. I am in tune with myself. I will reach this state of quiet, healthy being each time I do my alpha exercises. It will grow stronger and stronger each time I do it.

15. You will now begin your NEW programming. In your mind say I am going to leave the alpha state on the count of 5. When I open my eyes I am going to feel healthier and more relaxed than I have ever felt before.
    Now start counting slowly—in your mind—each number as you exhale. 1-2-3-4-5
    As you open your eyes on the count of 5 say—in your mind—the following:
    I am wide awake, free of tension, more relaxed and healthier than I have ever been.

You will be. The reason is that you cannot help being exactly that way because what you have done is to actually perform auto-hypnosis. While you were in that alpha state you gave yourself a post-hypnotic suggestion and your conscious mind had to obey that suggestion.

Now, perhaps you can understand exactly how you are going to change yourself and get rid of that artificial concept you've been carrying around all these years.

You will now be able to enter the alpha state each night before you go to sleep and insure a healthy, restful sleep. You will be able to enter the alpha state just before you wake in the morning and insure that you wake up alert, free of tension, full of real zest for living.

You can now—with the help of the alpha state—rid yourself of every habit you wish to break. Want to stop smoking? Stop drinking? Regain sexual potency? Whatever it is that you want to gain or get rid of, with relation to your real self—you merely have to command—and it will happen.

The post-hypnotic suggestions you give yourself must be obeyed. Any questions about yourself will be answered. Perhaps—before you command yourself to stop smoking— you might ask yourself why you smoke. The answer may surprise you. Also ask yourself why you drink—gamble—drive recklessly—eat too much.

HERE'S HOW TO QUESTION YOURSELF
WHILE YOU ARE IN THE ALPHA STATE:

I am going to wake up on the count of 5. When I do wake up I will know and remember the answer to this question: WHY DO I _____? Start counting—through 5 slowly. Then say, as you open your eyes, I am wide awake, feeling healthy and relaxed and the answer to the question is _____ (the answer will be there)

Each time you enter the alpha state your ability to achieve the alpha state will strengthen considerably. You will reach a point where you may give this post-hypnotic suggestion: I will be able to enter the alpha state merely by willing it from now on—whenever I want to.

I know this sounds like mumbo-jumbo but it works. That

means—at any time or place—where it is necessary for you to suddenly become super-calm and in complete control of all of your abilities—you will produce the alpha state instantly.

A sudden emergency will find you super-calm—able to quickly assess the situation and the right thing to do.

If you were at an important meeting and something came up that required a swift and correct decision you would be capable of doing that. With the advantages of your alpha state you will be able to use all of your potential any time you wish.

Your mental, physical and sexual powers will be far above the majority of people in the world because you will be one of the truly rare people capable of total function—total use of your talents, skills and potentials.

As you grow more adept at using your alpha state you will begin to see and hear much more easily. You will also 'see and hear' things that ordinary people cannot.

Most people around you will become obvious as children. You will know immediately whether people are telling the truth or a lie. You will see through people as easily as you can see through small children when they've done something wrong and are trying to hide the fact.

Just as you will know the truth about yourself and it will be impossible for you to lie to yourself again—so you will know the truth about other people and it will be impossible for them to lie to you without your knowing it.

As you progress you will gain greater freedom and your real self will be able to emerge completely and you will be happier than you have ever been before because you will be free for the first time in your life.

You will, at the same time, develop deep compassion for the people around you who are still held captive in their artificial self-concepts. You will find that you are able to influence people quite easily. People will gravitate to you—hang on every word you say.

You will have developed a power personality.

CHAPTER ELEVEN

LOOKING THE PART

In this chapter we are going to talk about your physical personality. This is a personality that is separate and distinct from your 'winning' or power personality.

Your physical personality is conveyed by your body. It speaks through your body. It cannot be hidden by beautiful clothes, furs, hair-styling, jewels or any other accessory. Like Shakespeare's description of murder—"though it has no tongue it speaks with miraculous organ."

If you happen to have the right kind of body personality you can wear rags and give the impression of a king or queen (depending upon your sex and inclination).

The first thing that has to be determined is—which do you have? The right kind or the wrong kind?

You know the answer to that question. There's no need to stand naked in front of a mirror. I would imagine that you have avoided that particular activity for some time now.

Well cheer up. Before you're finished with this chapter you will have the right kind of body personality.

Now before you wrinkle up your nose and start shaking your head—stop. Just reserve your final judgment for a little while. Listen to what I have to say—and then decide.

All right. I'm going to make some sweeping statements.

In fact, I'm going to make some outrageous statements. That shouldn't surprise you, by this time. I enjoy making those kind of statements mainly, I suppose, because I can offer you proof that they are true.

Now most of the things I am going to say will seem to contradict everything you have been told about exercise and dieting. Most of it is. Some of the things I will tell you do not contradict so much as they correct the degree of intensity.

For example: Any kind of violent or painful exercise is bad for you. That includes ordinary exercises that are pushed to the point of painfulness. I tell you that anyone who advises you to push your exercise to beyond pain is giving you the worst kind of advice.

There is a benefit to increasing simple exercises beyond your established comfort point but as soon as it gives you discomfort—stop, and walk around for awhile. Never stop suddenly and remain motionless—that puts a real strain on your heart because the muscles, which help to pump blood suddenly take away assistance to the heart and place a sudden burden on that organ. That's wrong. It's just as wrong as people who spring out of bed in the morning and engage in violent, prolonged exercise. They'll make one spring too many one morning and that will be that.

Later on I'll show you exactly how to wake up and exactly how to exercise in the simplest easiest way for maximum results and benefits.

Want some more nevers? All right, here's a list.

1. *Never jump into a cold shower in the morning.* It's not only masochistic—it's insane. The cold water clamps down everything, including your blood vessels. That clamping down can shoot your blood pressure sky high. It can deprive your brain of sufficient blood—cause you to faint—with the usual damage that occurs when you fall in a tub or shower. It could—in some cases—cause a heart attack. Don't do it. The best thing—in showers, as in life—is moderation.

2. *Never take salt tablets if you sweat profusely.* You don't need that much salt. Your system will go crazy trying to handle that large amount. It can make you nauseous—even make you faint. If you sweat profusely—drink water.

3. *Never do strenuous, sweat-producing exercises in non-porous clothing.* Your body must breathe. It must be allowed to reduce your body temperature to normal—naturally and without restriction.

4. *Never stand perfectly still for prolonged periods of time.* It makes your heart work all alone against gravity-drag without the assistance of muscle-blood pumping and can put a great strain on your heart.

5. *Never try to make up for lost sleep by oversleeping the next day—it doesn't work—it only hurts you.* The longer you stay in bed the more your body deteriorates. Take cat naps during the day and sleep less hours at night. You'll be amazed at the difference in your energy-output.

6. *Never hold your breath while you are lifting a heavy weight.* Breathe naturally while you are lifting. If you hold your breath you can build up internal pressure to a fantastic point—a bursting point.
7. *Never hold your breath and force a bowel movement.* The same reasons apply as for lifting a heavy weight. Incidentally—if you happen to be irregular—don't get in a panic and don't take laxatives. Try a shot glass of corn oil with your meals—you'll be amazed at the lubricated ease it will provide.

That's a sufficient amount of 'nevers'—let's go to some positive actions.

Our purpose, in this chapter is to give you a new body personality. So let's start putting your body in shape. That means exercising. Not the kind you're thinking of—the dull—boring and meaningless exercises you keep hearing about. I hate exercising for the sake of exercising.

I'm going to show you a simple series of simple exercises that you can do anywhere—anytime. They will—in an astonishingly short period of time—make you look and feel 1000% better than you feel right now.

Did someone say—why bother?

Good question. The reason is that your body talks to people without you're knowing it. It can shout 'loser' louder than you can shout 'winner'.

Your posture can weaken your power presentation.

I could go on with examples but just accept my word that your physical personality can cancel your winning personality as well as your power personality.

So let's start with exercises in the morning.

When you wake up—do not hop out of bed. Pretend that you are a cat. Ever watch a cat wake up? The first thing they do is yawn—I mean yawn! You'd think the edges of their mouth will touch their ears. It's a prodigious yawn. That's what I want you to do. Yawn for all you're worth.

The next thing a cat does is stretch—way out—right to each individual toe. That's what I want you to do in the morning. S-t-r-e-t-c-h way out. Then relax completely. Then sit up slowly, move your legs around until they hang over the bed—stretch your arms again—try to reach the ceiling while sitting down.

Then stand up—on your toes—as high up as you can. Stretch again—hands way up, over your head—reaching for the ceiling until you can feel that stretch right down to your toes and then—lower your arms slowly to your sides—settle down with your feet flat on the floor and relax your entire body. Roll your head around slowly like a rag doll.

That's it—exercise time is over—stroll to the bathroom with your fingertips pressed to your stomach (making a circle around your navel or belly button whichever you prefer). Keep your stomach muscles tense until you reach the bathroom then relax them for a moment, then tense them again while you wash your face, brush your teeth and so forth.

This, incidentally, is the start of a project known as 'getting rid of your pot belly'. Here's how:

Turn sideways (in the nude) and look at yourself in the mirror. Let you pot sag. Horrible, isn't it? Well do these two things: Lift your rib cage (chest) about an inch higher and tense your stomach muscles. Amazing—no?

Your pot has almost vanished.

I can hear you saying to yourself, "Does he expect me to go around, holding myself in like that, all day long?"

Yes, I do. The reason is quite sound. When you lift your rib cage and tighten your stomach muscles you improve your posture considerably.

Posture is power. The better your posture the better the image you project. Good posture denotes pride, power and confidence. Just think about that for a moment. Think about the men and women you've seen, in the office, at social functions, at the theatre, at any get-together. What was your first impression of a man or woman who displayed excellent posture; who stood erect and confident.

You were impressed with them, even though you were not immediately aware that it was the posture that did it. There was an air of poise and relaxed confidence about them, an aura of latent power. They were also sexually potent, as well. Posture is one of the ingredients in that magical aura called 'sex appeal'.

Men and women with good posture stand out from the crowd because the majority of people go around with a hunched over, 'whipped dog' posture and you dismiss them almost immediately. They just don't register in your mind and, if they do, they register unfavorably.

Here's a simple exercise that will help you to lose that unsightly 'pot' in short order. Women who have used this exercise, together with proper posture, have thrown away their girdles forever. Men who have used it faithfully have taken two to four inches off their waist and started to look ten years younger.

Just sit down, on the floor, and hook your toes under the couch, sofa or overstuffed chair in the living room. This gives you an anchor. Now clasp your hands behind your neck and hold your elbows in front of you, pointing towards your knees. Now do this exercise while counting in your mind. On the count of (1):

(1) Move forward and touch your knees with your elbows.

(2) Drop back slowly until your shoulderblades just touch the floor. Do not rest the weight of your body. Hold yourself in that lightly touching position for a full count of five—1,2,3,4,5.

(3) On the count of 5, raise your body slowly and smoothly until your elbows touch your knees.
Take a 2 count rest.

(4) On the count of 2, lower your body smoothly and easily until your shoulderblades lightly touch the floor, hold your position for a count of 5.

(5) On the count of 5, raise your body slowly and smoothly until your elbows touch your knees.
Take a 2 count rest.

Start this exercise slowly and easily and only do five (5) light floor touchings the first day. Each day thereafter add one additional floor touching until you have reached 10. Hold your exercises to 10. Do not overdo this exercise.

If you feel undo strain, stop, rest and then wait until the next day before resuming the exercises.

POWER POSTURE PRACTICE

Here's how I want you to practice walking from now on, wherever you are. Walk with your rib cage tilted upward, your stomach muscles tightened and your buttock muscles pressed inward. The way to make your buttock muscles behave is to place a half dollar between the cheeks of your buttocks and walk without dropping the half dollar. It will take a little practice but in a short while you will be able to hold that half dollar all the time. When you have familiarized yourself with the amount of tension it takes, you can discard the half dollar and just exert that much tension whenever you walk.

Now, at the same time you are tensing your stomach and buttock muscles your upper torso, shoulders and arms are completely relaxed.

As you begin to practice this type of walking a strange thing is going to happen. You are going to begin to feel healthier and more relaxed than you have ever felt before. A sense of power will grow within you and this aura of power is projected so that everyone becomes aware of it.

Do not, under any circumstances tell anyone what you are doing. Just do it faithfully and very shortly you will begin to receive comments from virtually everyone like,

"Hey! You look great! You really do."

Accept the compliment with a smile and a simple "Thank you," because it's a sincere compliment. You will look great. You will look poised and confident and you will feel that way.

After you've been consciously practicing that correct posture for awhile it will become second nature and you will do it automatically without thinking about it.

WEIGHT PROBLEMS

While this new posture will help considerably it cannot do the entire job. You're going to have to eat properly if you want to maintain a proper weight.

Contrary to popular opinions about the impossibility of maintaining your proper weight, there is a simple and perfectly natural way to do it.

First of all, let's eliminate an organic problem by having a complete physical checkup by your family doctor. If, after being checked out (which is a good idea to do every six months) you find that there's nothing wrong with you but too much excess fat, then you can start eliminating that fat quite easily.

There is only one basic reason for excess fat and that's excess calories. It's exactly the same as your financial balance sheet. If you spend more money than you earn you'll have a loss. If you spend less than you earn you'll have a profit.

Food—any kind of food—is fuel for your body. If you burn up more than you put into your body you will have a weight loss. If you burn less than your total food input you will wind up with an excess in terms of fat.

The easiest way to determine where you are in terms of excess calories is to use the 15 times method. That works this way. Weigh yourself on a scale. Let's say you're a woman with height and bone structure that should weigh 100 pounds. Using a general rule of thumb (this is NOT a perfect measurement because there are many other factors to be considered) you should not eat more than 1500 calories per day to maintain that weight. However your weight right now is 150 pounds which means you are consuming 2,250 calories or an excess of 750 calories per 24 hours.

Now there is a way to lose weight easily without changing one item in your regular diet. That is to change the time and proportion of each meal.

Here's what I mean. If you're like the majority of people you eat very little for breakfast; add more calories for lunch and have your heaviest meal at night.

That's exactly opposite to the way you should eat. Here's why. The greatest burn of energy (that means food/calories) takes place in the earliest part of the day. That's from the time you get up in the morning until about 1:00 in the afternoon. The next five hours are your secondary burn period. The following hours until bedtime are your lowest burn period.

Now if you could turn your eating habits around and eat the largest portion of your calories at breakfast, the next large amount at lunch and the least at dinner you would lose weight without changing a single item in your diet (supposing that you kept the calorie count the same during this period).

If you tell me that you just can't eat a hearty breakfast because you're just not hungry in the morning, I can well believe it. How could you be when you ate that heavy meal late at night and then did nothing to work off the excess? If you ate a very light supper and went to bed a little hungry each night, you'd begin to develop a ravenous appetite for breakfast.

Now before you tell me that you simply can't sleep if you go to bed slightly hungry, try this:

Drink a glass of milk (not too cold, please) a half hour before your regular bedtime. I guarantee that you'll become sleepy. Know why? Because milk contains a substance called tryptophane which is a sleep producing agent. It's most effective at night. This is also an excellent substitute for all those so called 'sleeping aids' which have been found wanting by the Food and Drug Administration in a recent study.

Now let's discuss your breakfast. First of all, fruit juice is an absolute must in the morning. For two reasons.

(1) A little fruit juice every morning keeps you regular. Incidentally don't worry yourself to death if you are not always regular as a clock. Temper, worry or anxiety can throw you off schedule from time to time. If the irregularity persists over a period of time—then see your family doctor about it. But occasional irregularity isn't anything to worry about. Do not use laxatives to excess because that can really throw you out of kilter.

(2) Fruit juice contains FRUCTOSE, a sugar used by the brain.

All right. Fruit juice is a must. Fresh fruit is even better. Have some on your cereal and, regardless of the kind of cereal, sprinkle some wheat germ on it. The wheat germ has a lot of Vitamin B-12 complex in it which is essential for your energy level and balance of emotions, oddly enough.

Eggs are an excellent source of protein and you can relax about the cholesterol charges because the medical community now feels that eggs are not bad for you unless you have an allergy or a medical problem.

You can have butter for breakfast if you eat it on wheat bread or have wheat germ on your cereal. Butter will digest better in the presence of wheat germ.

Do not rush your breakfast (or any other meal) eat calmly and enjoy your meal. Avoid angry arguments at any meal. Try to think pleasant thoughts while eating.

Now remember that there is a 5-hour rule of thumb. Approximately every five hours your body needs fuel. That means you'll be hungry 5 hours after breakfast. Suppose that you have breakfast at 5:00 A.M. Don't laugh, a lot of people do. In that case you'll begin to be hungry again around 10:00 AM—two hours before lunchtime. Instead of having a cup of coffee and a bun, bring an apple, orange, pear—what have you and eat that instead. You'll feel a lot better, it will take the edge off your appetite and it will feed your brain.

Now we come to that good old lunch period. Now think, for a moment. If you stuff yourself with a lot of starchy foods (particularly in the summer) you're going to be uncomfortable because you're going to be too warm. It's the same as suddenly making a big fire in the middle of the summer. All starchy foods begin to turn to sugar as soon as they hit your mouth. There are enzymes in your saliva which automatically turn starch to sugar. So the effect is almost the same as eating a bunch of candy bars.

Try a big chef's salad, instead. Sprinkle a lot of cheese on it and toss it a couple of times. The bulk will satisfy your hunger, the cheese will give you protein and the greens will do wonders for your complexion.

Now we come to supper. Try to avoid bread and butter. Potatoes are fine (without butter) eat lean meat, fish or poultry, lots of vegetables and, above all, make it a modest meal. Skip the dessert.

Try this kind of eating for a week and you'll be amazed at the difference it will make in your mental and physical condition. You won't lose a lot of weight (which is a no-no to begin with. Never try to lose weight fast.) But you will start to look and feel much better.

Incidentally you can never lose weight in a straight line of descent—even with those insane crash diets—because your body will lose some weight, then level off for awhile before it begins to lose weight again.

One of the reasons why you should never attempt a crash diet (starvation diet) is because your body needs protein every day. Your body cannot manufacture protein. It can manufacture carbohydrates from protein but it can't make protein out of carbohydrates.

So what happens is this: When you go on a crash diet your body begins to search for protein in order to stay alive as long as possible. It will remove protein from your muscles (which is why people look so horrible on those kinds of diets). However, when your body has used all the protein in your body it simply curls up and dies. Just like that. And the end can come quite suddenly without any warning other than the screaming of your raw nerves all the time.

So, please—no crash diets. All right?

EASY EXERCISING

I'd like to show you some easy ways to exercise all day long without appearing to. Walk is a vital exercise that too many people seem to avoid. Please walk to work if you can. Or if you can't do that, then walk stairs at every opportunity. For example, if you take a bus or subway to work, then get off a block or two before your regular stop and walk the rest of the way. You'll be amazed at what this will do for you after a few days. Also, if you work in a building with an elevator, get off a floor before your regular floor and walk up the one flight of stairs each morning. It will do wonders for your heart and put you in top form within a week.

During the day you can do a lot of quiet exercise without anyone noticing it. For example, when your phone rings, don't sit there and talk. Get on your feet and walk back and forth while you talk. If the cord is too short, have the phone company put in a long cord. It only costs a few dollars and it will pay you handsomely in a better looking body.

If you're in a plant or factory, every once in awhile, walk to someone's office to talk to them instead of just calling them on the phone or intercom.

Take a walk at lunchtime—to and from the place you usually eat at. Try to get some sun every day. It will help your body to convert the natural vitamins in your food. If you take vitamin supplements be sure to take them before you eat your breakfast or lunch. The few moments will allow the stomach acid to strip away the sugar coating so that the vitamins can be absorbed. You must take them just before meals because the food you eat provides the natural grounds for assimilating the vitamins. Otherwise you're just wasting your money.

When you get back from lunch, take 5 minutes and place yourself in a light alpha state. The calm you achieve will permit you to work easily and enjoyably for the rest of the afternoon.

At night, after your dinner, take the dog for a walk. If you haven't got a dog, take yourself for a leisurely walk (if you can't take a walk—do the dinner dishes).

If you continue to practice these simple exercises and start to eat properly; carry yourself erect with proper posture and muscle control; practice your alpha state exercises, a strange thing will happen. You will in addition to looking and feeling better than you ever have, also develop that rare look of serenity.

People are moved and fascinated by that kind of look. If you remember the television appearance of the Maharisi, the father of transcendental meditation, the one thing that everyone commented upon was his unique serenity.

This is exactly the kind of serenity you will develop as you begin to develop your new, physical personality. And all it takes is a little attention to your posture, to proper eating, and a few simple exercises. That's not too high a price to pay, is it?

Now all this will not give you a body as flamboyant as Miss America nor will it give you the muscles of an Olympic weight lifter. You really don't need either of those extremes. The body you will have will be a healthier and more attractive body and one that will operate for longer periods without fatigue.

You will have a much healthier complexion; your eyes will be bright and clear, and you will be physically and mentally alert at all times.

People will be fascinated by the easy fluidity of your walk and your relaxed, confident posture. You will also be aware of the gracefulness you have developed and the marvelous feeling of unlimited physical and mental power within you.

Another odd thing you will notice (and enjoy) is the fact that you will wear your clothes rather than the other way around. Naturally you will have an excellent wardrobe but even more importantly is the fact that you impart something special to everything you wear.

However, you must take special care with your grooming. I know it's difficult to do but you must make a special effort to maintain a clean, fresh look at all times. The power of a clean, fresh look is incredible.

I haven't said too much about your wardrobe other than telling you, earlier, that when I started out I bartered my services for a really excellent wardrobe. My clothes were very important to me and contributed to my fairly rapid rise to success.

There is an almost indescribable feeling of power that comes with wearing very expensive, beautifully created clothes. That sense of power and assurance is readily perceptible to everyone you meet. They are fully aware of how well dressed you are but they are more impressed with the aura of poise and confidence that you exude.

Clothes do make the man or woman. They are of major importance to you. They are not difficult to obtain. One of the simplest ways to get the wardrobe you want is to use a little misdirection.

For example. Let's make the finest store in your city the target. You will make your apparent objective the task of selling your particular services to the owners of that store.

Study the store, see exactly how your particular services would be valuable to the owner and then make up a strong presentation. Make it the best you can in terms of a visual as well as an oral approach.

Then make an appointment to see the owner or owners. Really sell your services. When you reach your closing—and you are told that everything is fine except that your price is too high (it should be high) then you can step in with the clincher. You can say,

"I really want you as a client—to the extent that I'm willing to accept my fee in clothing—and at retail—not wholesale."

Now that's an offer that most retailers cannot resist because it represents real savings to them. The difference between cost and retail price, as we explained earlier can be as much as 60%. In the essence you are actually putting money in their pocket.

They can arrange a line of credit for you against your retainer charge and you can have your super wardrobe in exchange for your services.

You should use this same technique with a top hair stylist and/or beauty parlor so you look superbly groomed.

There is virtually no avenue that you cannot penetrate with your service-barter technique and the ideal part is that when you have a large enough wardrobe you will then have a satisfied paying client if you have been delivering good and honest service.

Try to keep your hands and fingernails clean and well-manicured. There is nothing worse than grubby hands and ill kept fingernails.

You should have little trouble with body odor as you progress your diet and exercises. Your body will be healthier and more relaxed so you will not perspire as frequently.

To sum up, then, you have gained the keys to a 'winning personality' that will make people like you instantly. You have gained a power personality that will enable you to control and move people to do what you want them to do. Finally you have the key to creating a new physical personality that will enable you to 'look the part' and enjoy every moment of your life.

With these three, new assets in your hands you are ready to assume any role that you wish—or simply to enjoy your life more than you have ever enjoyed it before.

As I said, much earlier, once you assume your new role you will be 'on stage' for the rest of your life. This is not really as difficult as it may sound because as you continue to play your new role, you will find that the acting and thinking will begin to fuse together. Then, oddly enough, you will find that you have actually become the part you were playing. You will begin to relax and fully enjoy the new role you have chosen and it will become easier and easier for you.

Finally, you will reach the point where you will have a great deal of difficulty in remembering what you were like before you became the new, successful executive. The past will become a faint memory that eventually will disappear entirely and you will never return to it again.

The new person you have become, at that stage, will find that success comes easily because it is expected. People will like, admire, respect and love you because you will fully deserve that kind of treatment from everyone you meet. Isn't that the kind of life you want to live?

Well, it's in your hands now. You have to make the decision to go forward and become the kind of person you always wanted to be—or just remain where you are at this moment. It's your choice. No one can make it for you.

CONCLUSION

I could, at this point, give you a very interesting case history of any one of a number of people who have tried this blueprint and succeeded in becoming what they have always wanted to be. I decided against it because there is a really perfect example of someone who tried this method and succeeded.

I am that person. If ever there was a loser with almost everything in the world against success, I was the one. First of all, let's take the matter of being born on the wrong side of the tracks—that's bad enough, but to be born on the wrong side of the tracks—be poor—and be unattractive—well, that's a little heavy for anyone.

I started out with only one perfect asset—a burning desire to succeed—regardless of how much time and effort it took. It was a completely illogical desire because there just didn't seem to be any way in the world that I could accomplish what I wanted to do.

When I took stock of my assets they didn't amount to very much. I was a spindly, awkward little kid with a burning ambition and nothing else. That wasn't quite true. I could read. I had an excellent memory. When I put those two assets together with one of the finest library systems in the world, things began to click.

The more I read about success and successful men, the higher I raised my sights. I began to aim at the virtually impossible. Why not? Why restrict myself to small goals? Why not aim at the highest goal of all?

So I did. I aimed at nothing less than the absolute top. However I had read enough to know that aiming was one thing—getting there was another. So, while I kept my aim and goal as high as I could, I also began to plan on the steps that could take me there. Short, easy steps that anyone could accomplish.

The first step was a decent education. I knew that I couldn't get anywhere near my goal without it. My next thought was— since I was aiming at the top rung in a business career—maybe I should aim at the most prestigious school for business—that, of course, was the Wharton School at the University of Pennsylvania.

That, of course, was really reaching. How in the world would a kid like me, with no money, no friends, no social background ever get into a school like that?

You know how? By willing it to happen. One of the things I learned from a man named Napoleon Hill was this: If you lock your mind on a particular desire and keep it locked, day and night, without ever thinking that you won't make it—only that you will get it—it must happen.

There is nothing in this entire world that can withstand that kind of powerful, positive thinking. If you can hold that positive thought firmly and inexorably in your mind, it has to happen! Nothing can stand in its way. If it means that mountains have to be removed then mountains will be removed. Believe me, if I give you nothing else to take away with you—that thought is the most valuable gift I could possibly give you.

Don't take my word for it. Try it. With any kind of desire you wish. Just make it a specific wish—not a general kind of a wish like I want to have lots of money. Make it specific. Name the exact amount of money you want. It doesn't matter how much it is but in order to convince yourself that it works before you try to succeed with something that you will find hard to believe—try a sum of one thousand dollars.

Now just don't wish for it. Visualize it. See it in your mind. Start with ten one-hundred dollar bills. If you have never seen one or if you can't visualize one, go to the bank and get one. Study it. Back and front. Memorize it. Then start thinking about ten of them. See yourself, in your mind, laying them out on the table. Keep the thought on your mind continuously. See yourself counting each one-hundred dollar bill.

Now go one step further. Make a specific time when you will receive the one thousand dollars. Say, "I will receive that one thousand dollars exactly thirty days from today." Then start counting each day and have absolute confidence that the thousand dollars will arrive on that exact day. Look forward to receiving it with full confidence because it will arrive! Right on schedule.

Don't smile and shake your head in disbelief.

I can tell you from my own experience that it's absolutely true. That it can be done because I've done it again and again—not with thousands of dollars as my goal—but with millions of dollars! The sum of millions of dollars that I need for certain transactions has arrived exactly on the day that I wanted it to arrive. Right on schedule.

I was just as skeptical as you when I began to put that kind of power into practice. In the beginning I thought it was impossible for me to ever be enrolled at the Wharton School—and I was right! It was impossible because I believed it was impossible. When I finally decided to go all out and really started to believe that it was possible—and actually saw myself attending Wharton—and gave myself an exact date when I would enter Wharton—things began to happen. The rest is history. I not only attended that magnificent school—I graduated with honors.

However, even then, it was difficult not to begin to have doubts—to wonder whether or not it was merely a strange coincidence. I floundered for awhile after I graduated because I lost sight of the power of that kind of positive thinking. Luckily I got back on the track. I began to exercise that power—first in limited goals and then in bigger and bigger goals.

It didn't mean I didn't have to work hard—that doesn't change. But my specific goals were achieved each time. Why? Because I realized that I had to be alert and fully recognize the opportunity to achieve my desired goal when it arrived. That is the second and most important part of that power. You must be able to realize swiftly that the opportunity to achieve your desired goal has arrived.

Let's see if I can make that perfectly clear to you.

Take the thousand dollars that you fixed your mind on. It will not fly out of the air into your hands. Instead there will suddenly be an opportunity to earn a thousand dollars. An opportunity that would never have appeared if you hadn't fixed your mind on that particular desire.

The millions that I needed didn't fly out of the air into my hands. I was suddenly given an opportunity to obtain those millions by pledging valuables I already possessed. It wasn't a simple matter of offering those valuables to an investor or a banking firm—the firm or investor had to come to me.

Follow the blueprint in this book. Prepare yourself mentally and physically and place a desired objective firmly in the forefront of your mind—with a specific date—and move towards your goal with confidence.

Your opportunity will arrive—each time you specify your desire and the date you want it to happen. If you do your job to the best of your ability—and keep your positive power going—nothing in this world can stop you from becoming exactly what you want to become.

CASE HISTORIES

In the final stages of writing this book, we selected certain 'test readers' and gave each of them a copy of the final draft in manuscript.

Our criteria for selecting the 'test readers' was simple. We wanted readers that had little or no prior knowledge of finance; were at least 30 years of age; were demonstrably ambitious; had a steady income and, above all, had imagination.

We advertised and were astonished at the number of people who responded to our ad. Many of them, for one reason or another, were not suitable but we finally succeeded in putting together a team of five men and five women.

That we chose well was evidenced by the keen and perceptive criticism they provided after they finished reading the book.

They also provided something else—and added something that we had discussed more offhandedly than seriously.

My associate and I had both wondered, aloud, whether any of our 'test' readers would actually put the plan into operation. Then the press of work had put it out of our minds.

I promptly forgot about the conversation because a number of important meetings in the West and Midwest kept me busy for several weeks. There was no time (or need) to think about the book because it was in the hands of the publishers.

My associate, on the other hand, had been doing a lot of thinking about that conversation because the first thing he did when I returned was to hand me six manila folders and say,

"Before you open them, Steve, let me tell you something about them. Do you remember what we said, after the 'test reader' program—about whether any of them would try to put the plan into operation?"

"Yes, I remember that. You mean they did?"

"Well, yes—but you're getting ahead of me. I figured that some of them would and decided to gamble on it. I submitted the ten names to a clipping service and then put it out of my mind. The stuff you've got started coming in about a week ago."

I opened the folder on top and began reading. When I finished reading all of the material I sat for awhile, thought about it and then, after a discussion with my associate, decided to make some of the material a part of this book.

Both of us were aware that the publisher was going to scream like a wounded moose at the idea of adding this material to the book but we felt that it was important enough to stop production and re-do the book.

Obviously we have had to change the names to protect the people involved—not just from a legal standpoint (none of them have done anything illegal) but from the standpoint of courtesy and fair play.

Each of the people, that are presented in the case histories that follow, were interviewed by my associate, Donald Tyburn-Lombard. In each case he gave full assurance that their confidence would be respected. They are all aware that the case histories would be published but that it would be done without names or material that could, in any way, identify or embarrass them.

While it is a small sample to use statistically, it is interesting to note that six of the ten readers decided to try the plan. It is also interesting—although I hesitate to ascribe significance to it—that four of the six activists were women.

The case histories that you are about to read are based upon factual material. The substance has been derived from personal notes and from tape-recorded interviews conducted with each of the principals involved. I have tried to make these case histories as readable as possible without tampering with the basic facts. Certain things, such as actual names, places, etc. obviously have been altered for obvious reasons.

When the press clippings began to arrive I was pleased that the gamble had paid off. I read them, tucked them into manila folders and my only thought, at that time, was the amusement they would afford Steve, when he returned.

Then, as the clips began to mount up, another thought struck me. Why not interview each one of our activists and find out exactly what they'd done with the plan. I was certain that each of them had modified the plan in some way to suit the particular circumstances in which they would have to operate. There was also the talents and proclivities of the individual that would dictate a different course of action in each case.

So I was delighted when Steve decided to make the case histories a part of the book.

CASE HISTORY "MARY KAY"

My first interview was with Mary Kay, at her home (at her request) a well kept, unpretentious Cape Cod, in a pleasant suburban neighborhood about 35 miles from a fair-sized city.

My first impression of the house, from the outside, left me totally unprepared for the interior which was superbly decorated with remarkable appointments. She laughed at the expression on my face and shook her head in answer to my unasked question.

"No. You're wrong. I had all this before I started."

We had tea and a cigarette while I explained why I was there. She listened thoughtfully and then agreed to tell me the story with the understanding that I would let her read and approve of what I wrote before publication.

This (in essence) is what she told me:

"I answered your ad, not for the money, but mainly for want of something better to do. I guess I was at sixes and sevens with myself. Not really bored but just—in the doldrums—or maybe I was bored. I don't know. It was just a case of—why not?

The interview surprised me. I hadn't expected that. But you were very pleasant and it was all right.

If I had known there was going to be an interview I never would have gone. That's funny—in light of all that's happened. But I wouldn't have gone. I used to hate the idea of being examined like some kind of a bug. You know? Anyway—as I said—you were very nice so it really didn't matter.

Now the book—that was surprising. Well—you know how I felt about the book because you read my review—or was it a critique? Anyway—what you didn't know was that I dreamed about that damned book. I really did. I just couldn't get it out of my mind. I kept telling myself that it was ridiculous to go on mooning over the silly thing because I had no intention of doing anything like that. I have a comfortable income. I'm a widow and I'm perfectly content to remain a widow. I have two small children who are in school most of the day. My bridge club and my 'gray lady' activities at the hospital keep me active and occupied. There was no need for me to consider the idea.

But it persisted. I began to think about the fun of it. That's all—just something to play with—nothing serious. Not the car idea—although I think it's really sound—but that's more of a masculine idea.

I thought about the idea of having a completely furnished office at no cost. That intrigued me. I was a professional interior decorator before I married. After my husband died I thought about going back but, well—the children were younger then—and I was well off. Perhaps I just didn't want to get involved—it can be terribly aggravating you know.

Anyway—the more I thought about it—the more the idea began to take shape. When I actually sat down and began to sketch out ideas I knew that I was hooked.

So, one morning, after I dropped the children off at school, I drove into the city and arranged to have some business cards and letterheads printed up.

Then I began to drive around looking for suitable office buildings. You know, there were quite a few that didn't have an agent on the premises.

When my business cards were ready I started calling the numbers on my list. I had some difficulty in getting through to the owners until I tried a little deception. Instead of asking directly I would pretend that I was the secretary to the president and was calling to make an appointment with the owner.

I didn't have any trouble after that. Once, the owner of the building answered the phone himself and for a moment I didn't know what to say. Then I thought: what am I afraid of? I kicked myself into high gear and told him that I was the president of Corporate Management (not the name used) and that I wanted to see him about a mutually advantageous business deal. He asked me when I wanted to come see him and I said how about right now. He laughed, told me to come ahead and that was that.

His office was on the ground floor of a modern office building. He was acting as his own renting agent and I was delighted because it meant that he would be more receptive to the ideas I had.

He turned out to be a very decent man in his early sixties who listened politely and with not too much interest in my step-by-step plan until I said that as a 'bonus' incentive to prospective tenants I would offer professional interior decorating consulting without charge. He sat up then. When I added that I was prepared to assume the costs of advertising and promoting the buildings he began to nod vigorously.

It was a deal. In fact it was more of a deal than I had bargained for because he then told me that he had three other office buildings that he wanted me to take over. It seems that he'd gone on a building buying spree and had overextended himself somewhat. He was tired of running back and forth to the other buildings every time a prospect called. When I asked him why he hadn't used a real estate agency he shook his head and related some rather harrowing experiences he'd had with his first building before he'd moved in and took over renting it himself. I told him that I would be happy to take over all the buildings but that I wanted to prove out the first building before I took on the others.

I liked this man. He was honest and decent and I made up my mind that somehow I was going to rent his offices for him. I guess the challenge was beginning to take hold of me. I just knew that somehow I was going to do it—and I realized that if I did, I would make a considerable amount of money over the long run.

He had his secretary type up a letter of agreement and promised me a fully detailed contract later in the week; handed me a set of keys; a letter of authorization designating my company as renting agents and building management; the name of a good sign painter and wished me luck.

I drove back to 'my' office building in a state of absolute euphoria. I remember getting out of the car, standing across the street from the building, staring at it and imagining my name in neon lights right across the building. It was silly and childish but it was fun.

My euphoria didn't last too long, I think it evaporated when I took a look at the empty offices. The lobby was a disaster area. It looked like a big deserted, glass walled barn. I took out my notebook and began to write things down like: Is there any maintenance? Window washers—floor cleaners? I walked over to the wall register. Four tenants. The company names and room numbers were on a typewritten piece of paper. I felt so down I could have cried. It wasn't at all as I had imagined it would be. It was depressing and dirty and horrible.

"Then I started to laugh. I suddenly remembered what you'd said in the book about illusion. Everything could be changed. It just took a little imagination and some work. So what was I crying about?

I walked over to the elevator and surprise! It worked just fine. I rode up to the top floor because that was where I wanted to be—on top of everything.

The owner had already told me that the top floor was unfinished, except for the floors. As I stepped out of the elevator and turned, slowly, taking in the huge panorama without a lolly column in sight I suddenly had a vision of what a fabulous showplace this space could be made into. It made my head whirl until I thought of how much money it would take and I came down to earth with a thump! But the image remained and I began to really think about it. If there was a way to get the office space and the leased office furniture for nothing maybe—just maybe—there was a way to get the fabulous showcase for no money.

If only there was a way to construct offices without constructing them—and then it hit me! There was a way. There was a firm that sold or leased walls, bookcases, doors—everything—just like furniture. That was the answer. More than that—it means that I wouldn't be restricted to squares—I could employ the circle as a motif. I opened my notebook and began making little sketches with notes to remind myself of some of the ideas that were pouring through my mind.

Suddenly I wrote 'article'—because there was a terrific article in all this—maybe several articles—one for each of several trade journals. I might be able to get both valuable publicity and money for writing the articles.

I rode home with my head in the clouds, more excited than I'd been in a long, long time. It was a really heady experience even though I was aware that there was a lot of hard work ahead of me.

The next morning I called the owner and asked if the papers had been drawn up. He said that they hadn't been—but he would have them for me in a day or two, after he'd checked it all out with his attorney. I said that was all right. I'd go ahead with my authorization instead of wasting the few days.

He was pleased with my enthusiam and wished me luck and he really meant it. I told him that all I wanted from him—if the need arose—was confirmation that my firm was indeed the renting agent of record and building management. There was no need to go into the terms of our agreement. He told me not to worry, that he'd respect the confidence of the agreement.

I started checking through the yellow pages for office furniture leasing firms. I wanted the biggest one because what I intended would take a big firm. It would also take a key executive with imagination and foresight (as well as the power to make the decision).

When I narrowed the list to three firms, I sat down and began composing a letter. This was going to be a crucial operation and I wanted it to be just right.

The final draft of the letter was cool and right to the point. I opened by stating that I wanted a personal meeting to discuss a mutually advantageous business proposition; gave my corporate bona fides, and signed the letter with the first two initials of my name. I had no qualms in employing this harmless deception. If he was going to assume that I was a man—that was his privilege. If it caught him off guard when I walked in, so much the better.

As it turned out, the man that I eventually sold the idea to, knew in advance that M. T. Kay was a woman because he talked to the owner of the building. Oddly enough it was the fact that I was a woman that made him decide to see me. You never really know how these things work.

He bought the idea mainly from the standpoint of the publicity angle because he thought it was flaky enough (his words) to provoke an editor into running the articles. He also admitted that it was an excellent way to showcase his stock. Even more grudgingly he admitted that there was a possibility that I might be able to talk prospective tenants into a 'total' lease arrangement—particularly with the free interior decorator consultant as a bonus.

I didn't tell him but I also intended to hold out free publicity as a bait for my prospective tenants. Then, too, there was the gimmick of the 'art shows in the lobby' which I had already amplified in another direction.

My idea was to run 'Mini-Trade Fairs'—the basic scheme being to invite manufacturers to set up booth displays (on a non-competitive basis due to space restrictions) for a week-long mini-trade fair without any charge. Invitations would be issued to local businessmen (via a publicity campaign) and an interesting traffic pattern could be instituted.

This was not quite as simple as I thought because there was a question of liability insurance as well as a municipal permit but both were resolved satisfactorily in view of the 'no charge' aspect of the exhibitions.

One of the surprising aspects of my new activities was that previously I had all the time in the world but suddenly there didn't seem to be any time at all since I had to be back home by 3:30 when the children came home from school. Another was the fact that even though I was obtaining a lot of assets without money, it was still costing me money every time I turned around. However, the terms my lawyer had hammered out with the building owner not only gave me the entire top floor but, since I was arranging for the furnishing and lighting (that was a headache!) I was given sub-leasing rights for the space at my command on the top floor. That, as my lawyer pointed out to me, was a source of cash flow if I grabbed some tenants.

My lawyer, by the way was a tremendous help to me, but I persuaded him to find me a bright young lawyer for my day-today operation since I couldn't expect my family lawyer to continue giving me no-fee assistance. He did—but that's getting ahead of myself—the lighting headache, a really interesting problem that I never did think I'd be able to solve without spending a fortune.

You see the top floor had never been finished off because it had a truss type roof which meant a beautiful open space but also meant there was no ceiling and thus no overall lighting set up. There were only outlets in the wallboards—plenty of them but there would be nothing overhead until the offices were fully constructed and had ceilings over them.

My idea was that the offices would be constructed of movable walls—which would be installed like furniture and thus overcome the terrific construction costs (not to mention labor union problems). The office-furniture leasing company president was wild about the idea because he saw it as a revolutionary new way to enhance real estate values. That was something that I hadn't even considered.

He said that once we showcased the concept that it would change the basic structure of office buildings that would be built in the future. He'd already contacted a European manufacturer of modular walls and the head of the firm was going to fly over and work out the details personally—so it really looked as though things were going to move really rapidly.

Back to the lighting (I do ramble, sometimes) there was no possibility of putting up a ceiling because the cost would be astronomical.

It was the young lawyer who joined my firm that was responsible for the solution which was so simple it even astonished the wall man from Europe. The suggestion was to incorporate six by six foot lighting panels in each wall. The light would be even and because it would be on opposite walls there would be no shadows. Desk and floor lamps would provide the extra essential reading lights. We'd just ignore the lack of ceiling because that would merge into darkness up above. It was a brilliant idea and I was relieved because I had conceived of a wedge-formation for the offices so that they all converged on a central area very much like truncated slices of a pie (with a large hole cut out of the center).

I had a young photo-journalist working with us and he was taking pictures all over the place. I was going to work with him on preparing the articles and share in the profits with 70% going to him and 30% going to me. We already had 'go-aheads' from two magazines with tentative agreements from three others so we knew we had markets for the articles. The European wall man was going to get the articles for European dissemination without charge.

Everybody was full of enthusiasm as the offices began to go up. Meanwhile I was searching for tenants and I struck gold with a small employment agency that had to move to new quarters. A really nice and very smart woman headed up the agency and she signed up for two side by side offices and she suggested that her agency supply the girl-Friday who would man the central desk in the round foyer (with a phone console that would service all of the offices) which meant that I could offer a total reception service to all the tenants on my floor.

We had a long talk and the upshot was that she became an independent affiliate with my corporation and agreed to supply a member of her staff for rental representation in return for a rent-free status.

That was a wonderful break for me because I was beginning to seriously consider what kind of budget I'd have to set up for baby-sitters when things began to move. Remember I had agreed to have someone on hand at the building to service prospective tenants, five days a week from 9:00 A.M. to 5:00 P.M.

*   *   *

This was as far as Mary Kay had progressed which, in my opinion, is really moving along. I have no doubt that she'll really make it because she's enjoying every minute of what she's doing and that, in the long run, is what life is all about. Enjoy every minute that you live and you'll never have a chance to be bored.

CASE HISTORY "HENRY JAY"

The next case history is, on my estimation, something of a paradox. To be perfectly frank about it, I never really expected that Henry Jay would (or could) do anything with the plan. I'd chosen him, originally, as a sort of control in the experiment. I'd chosen him as the most unlikely candidate because I felt that if we could intrigue a type like Henry Jay we could hook anyone on the book.

Henry Jay was a rough and ready type with a voice that can only be produced if you have a sandpaper throat. While I realized that he had a certain amount of intelligence I really didn't think he was terribly bright.

Incidentally, this is exactly what I told Henry when I met him for the interview and he was delighted because that is exactly the way Henry likes people to see him. He says it gives him an 'edge' when people think that he's a perfect pigeon. I think I understand what he means.

Anyway, Henry's first question, when I called him, was "How much do I get for being interviewed?"

After the initial shock wore off I gently reminded Henry that he had appropriated the office copy of the manuscript which was worth (at the bookseller) about ten bucks.

He just laughed and told me to come over anyway. I must confess that I was a little apprehensive about Henry. It had been a shock (of disbelief) to receive a press clipping about him. A shock that was similar, I imagine, to the kind that a biologist would experience when he discovers that his 'control'—which was given a sugar pill instead of the vaccine—recovered beautifully from the disease. It was against all odds. Either I had seriously misjudged Henry or the book was a lot more potent than we realized.

Henry's office, in a rather new office building, was tastefully furnished. A willowy blonde, in a semi-detached dress smiled at me, squinted at my card and then whispered into an office intercom. She nodded then looked up at me and asked.

"One lump or two?"

"None, thanks. Just milk."

She smiled, stood up gracefully, crossed to the office door, knocked, opened it and ushered me into Henry's sanctum. I was impressed. Henry grinned at me from his desk (at least 20 feet from the door) waved me in and went on talking to someone on the telephone.

I sat down in a comfortable leather chair and listened to his performance on the phone. It was tight, taut, no-nonsense talk. When it was over, he grunted with satisfaction.

"Okay. What's on your mind?"

Before I could answer, the door opened and slender, tender and tall entered with two ornate coffee mugs. I accepted mine with thanks, took a sip and raised my eyebrows.

It was real coffee, not instant. Good, too.

Harry raised his cup in a salute. I nodded and took out my cassette recorder and put it on his desk. He shook his head slowly and scowled.

"Uh-uh. No tapes. Just talk between you and me."

"Why? What difference does it make?"

"The difference," he said slowly and seriously, "is the difference between direct evidence and hearsay."

I had really misjudged Henry.

"Why did you agree to see me?" I was curious now.

"I wanted to see the expression on your face when you walked in the door. It really grabbed you, didn't it?" He was grinning again and he reminded me of a picture of the big bad wolf standing outside the little pig's house.

"All right, Henry. I'm impressed. Want to tell me about it, or is this as far as you go?"

"Sure thing." He reached out, picked up the recorder, snapped out the cassette and began to rub his thumb along the plastic case as he talked.

"You know—your book was okay but it was too prissy. Too careful about legality and all that. You know?"

"And you're not? Is that it, Henry?"

"Not me. I'm legal all the way. Devious, maybe, but strictly legit. I got a lawyer that sees to it. You know?"

"All right, Henry—you're dying to tell me about your big deal—so why don't you?"

"Okay—this is the kind of a deal you should have put in that book. I mean the book is all right—but you got to have something a little different, you know what I mean? Okay, okay—after I got this office deal cooked up—which was dead easy, by the way—I started prowling around and I kept seeing these big empty lots with For Sales signs and a telephone number. It just seemed like there had to be something I could do about them. I kept thinking about it and thinking about it and then—wham! The whole thing came to me like it was ready-made.

I sat down and wrote a letter to three big, fast food outfits. Then I started calling up the people that owned these empty lots. I made appointments to see them and told them all the same story. I didn't know much about real estate or anything, I just had this hunger to own some land. I told them who I was and where I worked—didn't make any secret about it. But I told them this had nothing to do with my company—it was personal. None of them really believed me—which was okay because they were all sure that I wasn't too bright, you know? Well anyway, we'd fool around about the price, and I'd haggle but without too much smarts—and we'd finally settle on a price and I'd say okay, but—let me take an option on it for a couple of months.

"Then I acted surprised that it was going to cost me money for the option. So anyway, I'd give them a hundred or two hundred—whichever was the case and leave with an option to buy at the agreed on price. I remember this one guy he'd come down to $1,900.00 per acre on a forty acre parcel which meant a $76,000.00 deal—which wasn't bad considering that land was going to about $2,000.00 an acre only nobody was buying at the time.

"Anyway, before I was through I'd laid out a thousand dollars in options and I wasn't worried a bit because pretty soon I had my answers back from the fast food chains.

"I took the letterheads to a printer in another city and had them duplicated in color. Then I sat down and wrote a letter to each of the land owners.

"In the letter (which was from the real estate division) I explained that the property had been examined and was exactly what the company wanted to erect a new franchise operation. They offered a price that was $500.00 an acre more than the price quoted to me. It was a fair price.

"The letter went on to explain that above all they wanted no publicity—no loose talk about this offer. If word got out the deal was off. Now—if the deal was acceptable—they did NOT want to hear from him. If they didn't hear anything within three days they would assume that the deal was okay.

"A representative from the company, with a cashier's check would be visiting them and that would be that.

"Now what would you do in a situation like that? The letter was genuine. I used one of those re-mail outfits to see that the letter came postmarked from the city where the fast food chain had its headquarters. It has to be legit, right? So what would you do? Exactly what they did.

"I got a telephone call from each of those guys, the same day the letter arrived. After all, I'm kind of dumb, it shouldn't be too hard to separate me from my option, right? So I arrive, pigeon-toed and puzzled.

"Then I got the greatest bunch of song and dance stories you ever heard. One of them had the gall to tell me that there was a prior option which they hadn't known about so my option was null and void and here's your money back. Hah!

"Anyway the least I got was $500.00 and the most was $2,500.00 on the forty acre deal. I wound up with a little over ten thousand dollars for less than a week's work and an outlay of $16.00 for printing, postage and re-mailing charges. Now that's the kind of stuff you should put in your book."

"Didn't any of them realize that they'd been taken, Henry?"

"That's the funniest part of all! A fast food chain is opening up, but not in any of the locations I picked. So now they're convinced that I had nothing to do with it—just dumb luck on my part."

"You know what I think Henry?"

"What?"

"I don't believe a word of it."

"Why not?"

"Because if I print that story then every one of them will know that you pulled a fast one on them."

"Ah," he said with that foxy grin, "but they weren't being honest with me, were they?"

I had to laugh. I couldn't help it. Not one of them could say a word without admitting that they had been, to say the least, unethical.

We haven't heard the last of Henry, of that I'm sure.

*   *   *

I'd like to leave you with this thought: there is no need to engage in illegal or even unethical tactics. You can use the same amount of imagination and energy to get what you want legally and ethically—and you'll enjoy it more because it is legal.

If you should come up with some new wrinkle or idea we'd love to hear about it. Just write to Steve or me, care of the publishers.

SAMPLE STOCK CERTIFICATE

IMAGE
BUILDING
KIT

ABC TAX CONSULTANTS
Your address and telephone number here

STEVEN WEST
INVESTMENT COUNSELOR
Your address and telephone number here

UVISCO
CORPORATE MANAGEMENT
Your address and telephone number here

Steven West INTERIOR DECORATOR
Your address and phone here

CM
Telephone number
CORPORATE MANAGEMENT
Your address here

EDUCATIONAL MATERIALS CONSULTANT
Your address and telephone number here

LETTERHEADS

BUSINESS CARDS

ABC Your name and title
TAX CONSULTANTS
Your address and phone here

Telephone
STEVEN WEST
INVESTMENT COUNSELOR
Your address here

UVISCO
CORPORATE MANAGEMENT
Name and title
Your address and phone here

Telephone
Name and Title
CM CORPORATE MANAGEMENT
Your address here

NEWS for immediate release
(Your Company Name)
Address and Phone Number

Date:
Press Contact: Name & Phone

from: (your company name)
Address and Phone

press release

Date:
Press Contact: Name & Phone

from: (your company name)
Address and Phone

FOR IMMEDIATE RELEASE

Contact: (Name)
Phone; Date:

Address and Phone:

UVISCO Corporation

Telephone

Your address here

(Tint or color area)

customer's name and address

Date:
Invoice Number

YOUR ORDER NO.   DESCRIPTION

TERMS:

CORPORATE ANNOUNCEMENT

Federal's

FEDERAL'S INC.

Detroit, Michigan 48232

PRESS RELEASE

For additional information contact:
Mr. Steven West, Chairman of the board
313-869-7100

PRESS RELEASE FORMAT AND SAMPLE

FOR IMMEDIATE RELEASE
February 23, 1977

FEDERAL'S INC. Detroit, Michigan 48232

For additional information contact:
Mr. Steven West
Chairman of the board
313-869-7100

FEDERAL'S, Inc., a publicly held (OTC) Detroit based department store chain, announced today the sale of 1,250,000 shares of common stock to Federal's Management Corporation, a New York corporation. The stock represents approximately 25% of Federal's Inc. outstanding common stock.

In connection with the sale, Steven West was elected Chairman of the Board of Federal's Inc. and Mssrs. West, Herman Schneider and Jack Dashew were appointed to Federal's expanded Board of Directors. Maxwell Goldstein will continue as president and chief executive of Federal's Inc.

Steven West said, in part, "Our group is pleased to be associated with Federal's Inc. We believe there is potential for substantial business success. We intend to work with present management to expand Federal's operation. In addition to immediate financial strengthening, our group brings strong retail and financial experience to Federal's Inc.

We believe that this combination of resources and skills will cause Federal's Inc. to again become a strong force in the Detroit marketplace. We believe that Federal's Inc. will operate profitably in the next fiscal Year."

Steven West, the new Chairman of the Board of Federal's Inc. a publicly held, Detroit based chain of department stores, is also Chairman of several diversified companies. They include American Lease Industries, which operates 40 leased retail outlets; Toy Management Corporation operators of leased toy, sporting goods, health and beauty aids departments in the Federal Department Stores.

ABC
MANAGEMENT
a division of
UVISCO
is pleased to announce
the appointment of
JOHN DOUBLE, LL. B.
as legal counsel
and executive officer

CORPORATE
takes pleasure
in announcing

(YOUR NAME)
to the post of President

Name and title here

UVISCO

CORPORATE MANAGEMENT

Description
of
services
offered
here

Your address here

Name and title here

EDUCATIONAL MATERIALS CONSULTANT

Name and title

Your address and telephone number here

ABC

TAX CONSULTANTS
Your
address
here

STEVEN WEST

INVESTMENT COUNSELOR
Your address here

UVISCO

CORPORATE
MANAGEMENT
Address here

Steven West

INTERIOR
DECORATOR
Your address here

Steven West

INTERIOR DECORATOR

Your address and phone here

ENVELOPES

CORPORATE MANAGEMENT
Your address here

ABC TAX CONSULTANTS
Your address and telephone number here

STEVEN WEST
INVESTMENT COUNSELOR

Your address
and telephone
number here

UVISCO
CORPORATE MANAGEMENT
Your address and telephone number here

Steven West **INTERIOR DECORATOR**
Your address and phone here

Telephone number

CORPORATE MANAGEMENT

Your address
here

EDUCATIONAL MATERIALS CONSULTANT
Your address and telephone number here

LETTERHEADS

The various layouts of letterheads on this page are designed to provide you with variations which you may use to set up your particular type of business stationery. You may vary these samples as you see fit.

ENVELOPES

Always remember that envelopes are your 'first impression' sales representative and as such should be as presentable as possible. Try to have envelopes that match your letterheads.

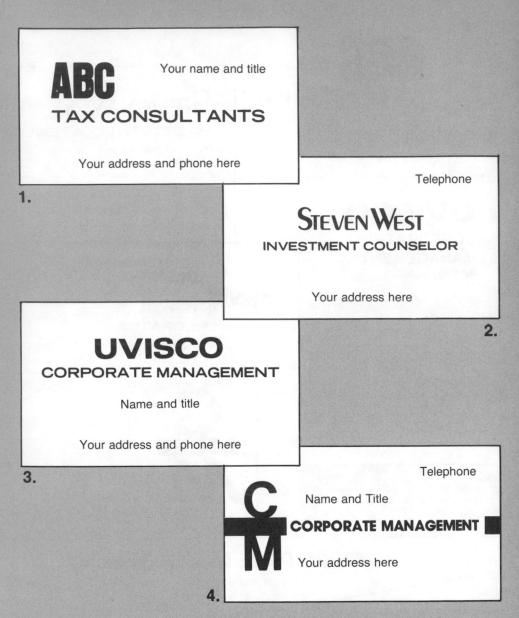

Business Cards are your personal representatives. They should have a crisp, fresh, intelligent look that suggests power and movement. Here are 8 different styles to choose from. Vary them as you wish.

1. Using your initials as the basis of your company logo.

2. This features your name if that's what you want to promote.

3. This type features your parent company. You become secondary.

4. Here you are using a symbol as the basis for your company logo.

5. This is the posh way ., with a crest repeated on the inside face of a fold-over card.

6. This variation offers a choice of a corner-cut or a round corner card.

7. Deckle edge is excellent for an 'arty' presentation.

8. Silk screened cards can give you a wide, solid color range of background.

Name and title here

CLOSED   **5.**

OPEN

Telephone

UVISCO

CORPORATE MANAGEMENT

Description
of
services
offered
here

Your address here

Name and title here

EDUCATIONAL MATERIALS CONSULTANT

Name and title

Your address and telephone number here

CORNER CUT   **6.**

ROUND CORNERS

DECKLED EDGE   **7.**

INTERIOR DECORATOR

Your address and phone here

SILK SCREENED 8.

NEWS for immediate release

(Your Company Name)
Address and Phone Number

Date:
Press Contact: Name & Phone

from: (your company name)
Address and Phone

press release

Date:
Press Contact: Name & Phone

from: (your company name)
Address and Phone

FOR IMMEDIATE RELEASE

Contact: (Name)
Phone; Date:

Address and Phone:

FEDERAL'S INC.

Detroit, Michigan 48232

PRESS RELEASE

For additional information contact:
Mr. Steven West, Chairman of the board
313-869-7100

PRESS RELEASE FORMATS

FOR IMMEDIATE RELEASE

February 23, 1977

FEDERAL'S INC. Detroit, Michigan 48232

For additional information contact:
Mr. Steven West
Chairman of the board
313-869-7100

FEDERAL'S, Inc., a publicly held (OTC) Detroit based department store chain, announced today the sale of 1,250,000 shares of common stock to Federal's Management Corporation, a New York corporation. The stock represents approximately 25% of Federal's Inc. outstanding common stock.

In connection with the sale, Steven West was elected Chairman of the Board of Federal's Inc. and Mssrs. West, Herman Schneider and Jack Dashev were appointed to Federal's expanded Board of Directors. Maxwell Goldstein will continue as president and chief executive of Federal's Inc.

Steven West said, in part, "Our group is pleased to be associated with Federal's Inc. We believe there is potential for substantial business success. We intend to work with present management to expand Federal's operation. In addition to immediate financial strengthening, our group brings strong retail and financial experience to Federal's Inc.

We believe that this combination of resources and skills will cause Federal's Inc. to again become a strong force in the Detroit marketplace. We believe that Federal's Inc. will operate profitably in the next fiscal Year."

SAMPLE PRESS RELEASE

AND PICTURE CAPTION

Steven West, the new Chairman of the Board of Federal's Inc. a publicly held, Detroit based chain of department stores, is also Chairman of several diversified companies. They include American Lease Industries, which operates 40 leased retail outlets; Toy Management Corporation operators of leased toy, sporting goods, health and beauty aids departments in the Federal Department Stores.

UVISCO Corporation

Your address here

(Tint or color area)

customer's name and address

Date:
Invoice Number

YOUR ORDER NO.   **DESCRIPTION**

TERMS:

INVOICE

ENVELOPE

UVISCO Corporation
Your address here

INVOICES
This, too, is a projection of
your company's overall image.
The design shown here gives
you that important image and,
saves you time and money
because there is no need to
type an envelope. Just slide
these filled out invoices into a
window envelope and the
customer's name and address
are clearly visible.

customer's name and address

ABC

CORPORATE MANAGEMENT

a division of
UVISCO
is pleased to announce
the appointment of
JOHN DOUBLE, LL.B.
as legal counsel
and executive officer

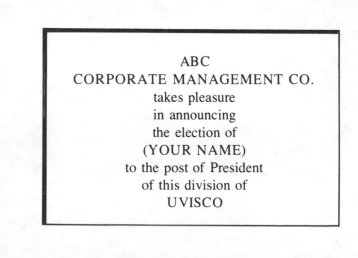

ABC
CORPORATE MANAGEMENT CO.
takes pleasure
in announcing
the election of
(YOUR NAME)
to the post of President
of this division of
UVISCO

SAMPLE STOCK CERTIFICATE

For Value Received,_____ hereby sell, assign and transfer unto

PLEASE INSERT SOCIAL SECURITY OR OTHER
IDENTIFYING NUMBER OF ASSIGNEE

_____ Shares
represented by the within Certificate, and do hereby
irrevocably constitute and appoint
_____ Attorney
to transfer the said Shares on the books of the within named
Corporation with full power of substitution in the premises.

Dated _____ 19___

In presence of

_____   _____

NOTICE THE SIGNATURE OF THIS ASSIGNMENT
MUST CORRESPOND WITH THE NAME AS WRITTEN UPON THE
FACE OF THE CERTIFICATE, IN EVERY PARTICULAR, WITHOUT
ALTERATION OR ENLARGEMENT, OR ANY CHANGE WHATEVER

BACK OF STOCK CERTIFICATE

These new books can

MENTAL CALISTHENICS

Here's an exciting book that offers you a 30 day How-To Program of mental exercises that combine the techniques of meditation, yoga, psychoanalysis, primal, transactional analysis, written in swift-reading language. Steven West, the well known psychologist and author gives you step-by-step instruction in this easy-to-read book. **$9.95**

- Learn How To Use The Alpha Dimension
- Understanding Your Strengths And Weakness
- Learn How To Use Body Language
- Understand How To Change Your Programming
- Learn How To Eliminate Bad Habits Easily
- Understand How To Approach Sex Positively

BONUS: Long Playing Record That Teaches You How To Use The Alpha Dimension.

WHAT HAPPENS AFTER DEATH?
You Don't Have To Die To Find Out

Now, for the first time, you can learn the entire truth about Life and Death. Here, in one easy-to-read volume you will find the answers to many of the questions that have puzzled and frightened you over the years. Here is a book that will enlighten you and comfort you more than any book you have ever read **$9.95**

- Truth About The Origin Of Man
- New Evidence About Reincarnation
- Cases Of People Dying And Returning
- Out-Of-Body Experience Reports
- Mythology, Magic and Religion
- Visitors From Outer Space/UFOS
- Mysterious World Of Dreams

BONUS: Actual Coin Replica of PERSEPHONE The Goddess Of Returning Life

---

Your tape player can become a learning machine

HOW TO STOP SMOKING IN 30 DAYS

Here's a complete, step-by-step program on a cassette that you can play on your cassette player and learn how to stop smoking swiftly, simply, easily. This new program uses a combination of mental exercises, meditation and behavior modification that will release you from your smoking habit in 30 days time! **$9.95**

- You'll Feel Better, Look Better, Live Longer!
- You Will Not Gain Weight With This Program!
- Your Smoker's Cough Will Disappear Forever!
- You Won't Feel Frustrated Or Strung Out!
- You'll Breathe Easier, Sleep Better!

NEW PERMANENT WEIGHT LOSS PROGRAM

Now, for the first time, here's a program that you can play on your cassette player that will teach you how to lose weight easily, swiftly, permanently! Steven West, a leading psychologist and author combines the techniques of meditation, psychology and nutrition in a new, permanent, weight loss program that you can use immediately. **$9.95**

- Quick Results With Weight Loss Of 3 to 4 Pounds Each Week You Continue This Program!
- This Is An Easy Program — No Complicated Calorie Counting Or Expensive Time Consuming Gadgets!
- Improve Your Health At The Same Time You Begin To Look Better, Feel Bettery Day By Day!
- Gain New Energy, New Relaxation, Find A New Zest For Life And A Better Outlook On Life!

change your life!...

HOW TO LIVE TO BE 100 AND ENJOY IT!

There is a way for you to add 30-40 or 50 happy, vigorous, healthy years to your life span! This book tells you how to live better now and in the years to come. It offers you a complete, detailed program that you can put into operation immediately so that in less than 30 days you can start to look and feel years younger!   **$9.95**

- **Understand the RNA-DNA — No Aging Diet**
- **How To Conquer Your Dangerous Tensions**
- **Life Force and the 17 Rare Live Foods**
- **Sexuality and Alpha Waves Expand Life**
- **Secrets of the Hunzas — Live to 125**
- **60 Second Heart Exercise To Keep Young**

BONUS: WEIGHT CONTROL SUPPLEMENT
3000 Different Foods Evaluated

THE POWER & PLEASURE OF SEX

Now you can release the passionate, uninhibited lover that's been trapped inside you all your life! Here, in a unique new book is the knowledge you have been looking for! It's a completely new and different approach to sexual relations which, will for the first time permit you to become the lover you have always wanted to be.   **$9.95**

- **Acting Out Your Sexual Fantasies**
- **Primal Sensuality Discoveries**
- **Getting To Know The Nude You**
- **Developing Your Sensual Nature**
- **The Art Of Self Exploration**
- **Writing Your Sexual Biography**
- **Giving/Receiving Love Massage**

BONUS SUPPLEMENT: ANALYSIS OF THE
KINSEY/MASTERS & JOHNSON/HITE REPORT

AMW
Aabbott McDonnell-Winchester
376 Wyandanch Avenue
North Babylon, New York 11704

Please send me the following books (cassettes) @ $9.95 each plus 95¢ for postage and handling.

☐ Mental Calisthenics
☐ What happens after death
☐ Live to be 100
☐ Power & pleasure of sex
☐ Stop smoking in 30 days
☐ Permanent weight loss

☐ Check enclosed   ☐ Charge my credit card;
☐ Master Charge card ☐ BankAmericard Exp. Date _____

Card # _____

Name _____

Address _____

City _____

State _____ Zip _____

New York residents add 7% sales tax.